Grant
from mom
3/30/07

a first book of
Japanese cooking

Masako Yamaoka

KODANSHA INTERNATIONAL LTD.
Tokyo, New York, and San Francisco

The publisher would like to thank the following for donating tableware: Savoir Vivre, Seibu Department Stores, Ltd., and Tachikichi Inc.

Ingredients on pages 23 and 24 were supplied with the cooperation of House Food Industrial Co., Ltd., JFC International Inc., and Kikkoman Corporation.

Photographs by Tamihisa Ejiri

Distributed in the United States by Kodansha International/USA Ltd., through Harper & Row, Publishers, Inc., 10 East 53rd Street, New York, New York 10022.
Published by Kodansha International Ltd., 12-21, Otowa 2-chome, Bunkyo-ku, Tokyo 112 and Kodansha International/USA Ltd., with offices at 10 East 53rd Street, New York, New York 10022 and at The Hearst Building, 5 Third Street, Suite 430, San Francisco, California 94103.

Library of Congress Cataloging in Publication Data

Yamaoka, Masako.
    A first book of Japanese cooking.

Includes index.
    1. Cookery, Japanese.   I. Title.
TX724.5.J3Y2764 1984   641.5951   84-80161
ISBN 0-87011-659-2 (U.S.)
ISBN 4-7700-1159-8 (in Japan)

CONTENTS

Preface

For over thirty years it has been my great pleasure to teach home-style Japanese cooking to Japanese and other peoples of various nationalities. Many of my foreign students have become my friends, and it thrilled me to realize that they would one day take what they learned back home to countries throughout the world.

Over the years as I traveled abroad, I have been delighted to meet friends and former students—all of whom still displayed an eagerness for Japanese food—and to see authentic Japanese dishes brought into homes everywhere. This in itself is reward enough for one lifetime.

Several years ago I was invited by my former-student-and-now-friend Mrs. Kathryn A. Fischbach and her husband to visit and teach in the United States. Here, too, I met with heartwarming enthusiasm for my national cuisine. While in Boston, we searched for a good English-language book on Japanese food, but, much to my surprise, what few we found were disappointingly inadequate for our purposes.

I have seen that good, wholesome Japanese food may be enjoyed anywhere. Ingredients are plentiful in major cities and are available with increasing regularity in smaller cities and towns. Sensible home cooking is responsible for the health and well being of the entire family and promotes enjoyment at the dining table, the hub of the family. Variety, flavor, visual appeal, and health—all these are undeniable reasons for cooking Japanese.

Cooking for family and friends has always given me much satisfaction, and this pleasure has been multiplied countless times by thoughtful letters from friends and former students expressing their continued enchantment with Japanese food. I hope this book captures the essence of the dishes they enjoy and that it enriches the lives of everyone, anywhere, who cooks with love.

I would like to dedicate this book to Mr. and Mrs. Daniel L. Fischbach who first inspired me with the idea for doing a book, their parents Lieutenant Colonel and Mrs. Robert W. Flanagan, and Ann Curtis, who devoted herself wholeheartedly to this project. Thanks also go to Therese Shaheen, all my foreign friends, and my assistants. Lastly my special thanks and appreciation to Katsuhiko Sakiyama, Michiyo Kashiwagi, and Barry Lancet, my editors at Kodansha International.

Masako Yamaoka

top to bottom: Egg-drop Soup (page 36), Shrimp and Asparagus
Soup (page 38), Miso Soup with Mixed Vegetables (page 40),
Miso Soup with Tofu and *Wakame* Seaweed (page 39)

top to bottom: Miso-stuffed Trout (page 55), Yellowtail Teriyaki (page 54), Sashimi Platter Supreme (page 51)

"Riverbank" Oyster Pot (page 56)

top to bottom: Ginger Pork Sauté (page 70); Chicken Roll (page 62); Beef Tartare, Japanese Style (page 69)

Shabu-shabu (page 64)

top to bottom: Egg "Tofu" Custard (page 76), Savory Dinner Egg
Custard (page 77), Thousand-layer Rolled Omelette (page 74)

12

top to bottom: Chilled Fresh Tofu (page 81), Deep-fried Fresh Tofu and Eggplant (page 83), Grilled Tofu with Three Toppings (page 84)

top to bottom: Baked Eggplant (page 88), Lemony Squash (page 87), Simmered Chinese Cabbage and Deep-fried Tofu (page 89), Turnip Cups with Miso Sauce (page 90)

top to bottom: Green Beans with Sesame Dressing (page 98),
Five Vegetables with Tofu Dressing (page 98), Crab and
Cucumber with Golden Dressing (page 96)

15

Green Pea Rice (page 104)   Mixed Rice (page 105)

Udon Noodles in a Pot (page 111)

Cucumber Pickles (page 115)

Lemony Pickled Turnips (page 115)

top: Strawberries in Bubbles of Snow (page 118)
bottom: Sweet Potato Purée with Chestnuts (page 119)

counterclockwise from top right: Soft Simmered Chicken Gizzards (page 44), Skewered Chicken Quenelles (page 43), Chicken-stuffed Squash Balls (page 44), Pork and Vegetable Kebabs (page 46), Smoked Salmon and Daikon Rolls (page 42), Shrimp Sushi (page 47)

Tempura (page 138)

counterclockwise from top left: Salmon and *Shiitake* Mushroom Sushi (page 124), Mixed Sushi Bowl (page 133), Thick Roll Sushi (page 126), Cherry Blossom Sushi Roll (page 129), Thin Roll Sushi (page 125), Sushi in a Purse (page 131), Do-it-yourself Sushi (page 121)

top: Green Pea Rice (page 104)
bottom: Mixed Grill (page 66)

21

1. through 3. various misos 4. low-salt soy sauce 5. dark "regular" soy sauce 6. artificially brewed *mirin* 7. naturally brewed *mirin* 8. rice vinegar 9. saké 10. instant kelp stock (liquid) 11. instant bonito stock (liquid) 12. bonito flakes 13. powdered *wasabi* horseradish 14. hot yellow Japanese mustard 15. ready-to-use grated ginger 16. ready-to-use *wasabi* horseradish 17. *sansho* powder 18. ground red pepper 19. seven-spice mixture 20. instant bonito stock (granules) 21. cellophane noodles 22. dried *soba* noodles 23. *somen* noodles 24. fresh cooked *udon* noodles 25. dried *udon* noodles

1. freeze-dried tofu 2. thick deep-fried tofu 3. thin deep-fried tofu 4. "silk" tofu 5. "cotton" tofu 6. *okara* (tofu pulp) 7. "instant homemade tofu"

1. agar-agar bar 2. agar-agar powder 3. dried kelp 4. *wakame* seaweed 5. *nori* seaweed 6. dried gourd ribbons 7. dried *shiitake* mushrooms 8. white sesame seeds 9. black sesame seeds

1. burdock 2. daikon radish 3. lotus root 4. Chinese cabbage 5. canned lotus root 6. canned burdock 7. canned bamboo shoots 8. fresh whole bamboo shoot 9. fresh ginger 10. *enoki* mushrooms 11. fresh *shiitake* mushrooms

INGREDIENTS

Happily, basic ingredients for Japanese cooking are now available at a constantly growing number of supermarkets and healthfood stores. Moreover, in order to meet the rising demand, many fish, vegetable, and meat markets now offer Japanese products to supplement the sashimi, daikon radishes, sukiyaki-cut meat, and the like they have begun selling. Further, the number of oriental markets is rapidly increasing. Chinese and Korean stores frequently have a selection of Japanese goods, since the demand is on the upswing and distribution systems are expanding. At the very least such stores stock ingredients such as dried *shiitake* mushrooms and cellophane noodles. Low-cost import emporiums are a good source of canned and dried goods; that is, products that have a long shelf life.

The following guide contains notes on how to recognize high-quality goods and distinguish freshness, as well as storage instructions and length of time perishables and nonperishables will keep. Japanese names are indicated along with any other variation in either language. Jotting down the alternate names in addition to the Japanese names will make shopping easier the first time out. Mail order inquiries are also possible, and so a list of outlets is provided in the appendix (pages 151–53). See color plates (pages 23 and 24) for representative examples of Japanese ingredients.

agar-agar (*kanten*)

A jellying agent extracted from *tengusa* seaweed, agar-agar congeals quickly and unmolds from smooth surfaces with ease. In addition, it holds a shape as well as gelatin and does not have the rubbery toughness. Powdered agar-agar may be found at supermarkets and healthfood stores, whereas Japanese and Chinese provision outlets carry the bar form as well. (Other forms of agar-agar are also available, but potency may vary.) The potency of 1 bar remains basically unchanged, even though the dimensions (approximately $10 \times 1\frac{1}{4} \times 1\frac{1}{4}$ inches/ $25 \times 3 \times 3$ cm) sometimes vary. Bars dissolve when boiled in water. See page 117 for preparation of bars.

bamboo shoots (*takenoko*)

Canned bamboo shoots are easily found at Japanese and Chinese oriental outlets, supermarkets, and import emporiums. Bamboo shoots must be washed well and any grainy white residue removed. Once opened, they will keep for at least 4 days refrigerated in a sealed container filled with fresh water or can liquid. Change water daily. Instructions are for sliced, not whole, shoots since sliced are more common; however, whole shoots work just as well. Amounts given in recipes are dry measure.

bonito flakes (*hana-katsuo* or *kezuri-bushi*)

These thin, light brown shavings are one

of the two basic ingredients for bonito stock (pages 35–36), the foundation of much Japanese cooking. Originally flakes were shaved daily from rock-hard dried bonito fillets. Today packaged flakes are used throughout Japan in most homes and restaurants. Instant bonito stock products that admirably capture the essence are also acceptable substitutes and are widely used in Japan. For more information, see note on page 35.

Flakes are also used as a condiment for various tofu dishes, as a flavor garnish with vegetables (such as cucumber or watercress in Do-it-yourself Sushi), and so on. Instant liquids or granules cannot be substituted in these cases. Put flakes in an airtight container and keep away from moisture. Instant products should be refrigerated after opening.

burdock (*gobo*)

Available fresh or canned at most oriental food stores, this seasonal root is used to advantage in soups and simmered foods. Its appeal lies in its carrotlike crunchiness and its ability to absorb flavors. Look for rock-hard specimens that have unwrinkled skins.

Fresh burdock should be scrubbed well with a stiff brush to remove clinging dirt but never scraped or peeled, since the thin skin contains much of the flavor. Fresh burdock quickly looses its whiteness once it is cut, so soak it in a generous amount of water or water with a dash of vinegar for at least 10 or 15 minutes to prevent discoloration.

Fresh burdock keeps 2 weeks refrigerated if wrapped in plastic or newspaper. Canned burdock, once opened, keeps 4 to 5 days refrigerated (2 to 3 in summer) with can liquid in a sealed container. Recipes are for fresh burdock. If using canned burdock, skip scrubbing, soaking, and parboiling.

cellophane noodles (*harusame*; "spring rain")

Search for thin, dried white or translucent noodles that do indeed look like spring rain and you will soon find these noodles, which are stocked at both Chinese and Japanese stores. Though technically "filaments," they are consistently packaged and sold as "noodles." They are often labeled "transparent noodles" and sometimes called "pea starch noodles" or some such. Do not confuse them with thin rice noodles, which have a similar appearance at first glance. Before using, noodles should be soaked in warm water until soft (10–20 minutes). High-quality noodles will not break into pieces when cooked.

Chinese cabbage (*hakusai*)

This versatile, greenish-white leafed cabbage is used in stir-fry and one-pot dishes, added to soups, and made into pickles. A heavy, succulent vegetable, Chinese cabbage is often found in supermarkets, not to mention oriental food stores. It is also known as "celery cabbage" and "nappa (sometimes 'Napa') cabbage." Avoid produce with spotted leaves, if possible. Store as you would lettuce.

cucumbers

Recipes in this book call for American cucumbers, which are equivalent to 2 or 3 Japanese cucumbers. In general, peel and seed cucumbers unless skin is delicate and thin and seeds are immature. If using the small Japanese variety, it is not necessary to peel or seed cucumber. However, to smooth the rough surface and bring out the skin color, dredge cucumber in salt and roll back and forth on the cutting board several times with the open palm. Wash well.

daikon radish (giant white radish)

This long cylindrical giant radish is surfacing with increasing regularity in the vegetable sections of major supermarkets in the United States. In addition, since it is of primary importance to Japanese cooking, it is stocked in most Japanese food stores. Large white radishes or ordinary turnips are acceptable substitutes. The former is the better alternative if finely grated radish is called for.

Always remove the thick skin before cutting or grating daikon. To grate daikon and for information on Japanese graters made especially for that purpose, see page 141. Grated daikon will keep about 3 hours refrigerated before becoming soggy. Choose daikon radishes with firm, tight skin and avoid those with soft or wrinkled skin. Keeps 2 weeks refrigerated.

eggplant

Eggplants used here are the 6-inch (15-cm) specimens that weigh approximately 10 oz (285 g) each, rather than the small Japanese eggplants that are on the average 4 inches (10 cm) long and weigh 2 to 3 oz (60 to 90 g). Because size varies by region and season, weights have been included to offer a guideline. If using the small Japanese variety, substitute 3 to 4 eggplants for every eggplant in these recipes, again using listed weight as a guide.

ginger, fresh (*shoga*)

Fresh ginger is sold in many supermarkets, and certainly in any Japanese, Chinese, or Korean food market worth its title. Look for ginger that has large knobs, is firm when pressed (not soft), and has smooth, unshriveled skin without dark discoloration. Tubes of ready-to-use "fresh" grated ginger are also available.

Fresh ginger contributes immeasurably to the overall flavor of any dish it is used in, so do not substitute dried or powdered ginger, or any other variant. Ginger is easily stored for long periods by freezing it unwashed, unpeeled, and unwrapped. Break off pieces as needed and return remaining ginger to the freezer compartment. Refrigerated, fresh ginger keeps 2 to 4 weeks wrapped first in a paper towel or napkin and then in plastic wrap.

Ginger juice: Wash fresh ginger root well to remove any clinging or trapped dirt (or peel the amount you need). Place cheesecloth or paper towel over a small bowl. Grate ginger over bowl, using the finest surface on your grater. Gather up ends of cheesecloth and squeeze out juice. Juice may also be obtained by grating ginger and squeezing grated material with your fingers.

To grate ginger, follow directions for ginger juice (see preceding paragraph) but do not squeeze. For information on Japanese graters specifically for grating ginger, see page 141. See following two entries for vinegared ginger.

ginger, red vinegared (*beni-shoga*)

This bright red vinegared ginger acts as a flavoring agent in Thick Roll Sushi (page 126), is a coloring agent in Cherry Blossom Sushi Roll (page 129), and performs both duties in Mixed Sushi Bowl (page 133). It is available ready to use in the refrigerated section sealed in plastic packs or on the shelf in small bottles. It will be found alongside sweet vinegared ginger, which is pink (not red).

ginger, sweet vinegared (*amazu-shoga*)

This thinly sliced pink (not red) ginger is almost exclusively used as a garnish and is frequently served with sushi and other dishes to refresh the palate. Sweet vinegared ginger is available at most oriental outlets sealed in plastic packs. Drain well before using. Once opened, store-bought ginger keeps 3 to 6 months refrigerated in a sealed container with package liquid.

Sweet vinegared ginger is easily made at home. Peel 1 1/2 to 2 oz (45 to 60 g), or about 2 inches (5 cm), fresh ginger and slice paper thin. In a small saucepan bring 1 to 2 cups water to a rolling boil, add 1/2 tsp salt and sliced ginger, and continue to boil over high heat for 1 minute. Drain.

Combine 1/4 cup rice vinegar and 3 Tbsps sugar, add ginger, and set aside. Ready as soon as 1 hour but best after 4 or 5 hours. To serve, drain well and mound decoratively on plate. Homemade sweet vinegared ginger keeps 7 to 10 days refrigerated if stored in sweet vinegar solution. Store-bought products keep longer.

gourd ribbons, dried (*kampyo*)
The flesh of a variety of large calabash gourds is peeled off in long strips and dried. Small (1 oz/30 g) packages are available at most Japanese food stores. Dried gourd ribbons vary in quality, so choose white or buff-colored specimens (avoid yellowish ones) that have an even thickness throughout and are on the spongy, rather than dry, side.

To use, rinse under cold running water and scrub with salt, soak until soft (about 30 minutes), and then boil, adding flavoring ingredients as directed. Cooked gourd ribbons keep 2 to 3 days refrigerated. To store dried gourd ribbons, wrap first in newspaper (or paper towels) and then in plastic wrap, and refrigerate or store in cool dark place. Dried gourd ribbons keep 1 year.

kelp, dried (*konbu*)
Kelp stock and kelp-seasoned broth (or water) serve as a base for many dishes, and the latter is a main ingredient for bonito stock (pages 35–36). Good-quality kelp will have thick, flat leaves, be an opaque greenish black or brownish black, and have a fine white powder. Poor-quality products are thin , wrinkled, and green or reddish. As with *nori* seaweed, price is also an indication of quality. Buy whole long strips and avoid kelp pieces, if possible.

Contrary to what general-purpose manuals might say, do not wash or rinse kelp, but instead lightly wipe both sides with a damp cloth. The fine white powder contains much of the flavor and should be left intact. Store *konbu* in an airtight container. Keeps a long time.

lotus root (*hasu; renkon*)
Fresh unblemished specimens are hard to find in the United States, so recipes in this book call for canned (boiled) lotus root, which retains much of the flavor and the toothsome crunchiness. However, it is worth keeping an eye out for the raw root, and, if you are lucky enough to find fresh lotus, look for firm, unbruised roots that have thick flesh and small holes with undarkened inner walls.

Once cut or scraped, lotus root, like burdock, discolors quickly, so after cutting, immediately put it in water with a dash of vinegar until ready to use. When using fresh lotus, scrape, cut, and soak, then prepare the root in the same manner as other raw vegetables with a similar firmness (carrot, burdock, etc.) are prepared in the recipe being followed. However, cooking time for fresh lotus is less than that of burdock and carrot.

Whole links should be wrapped in damp newspaper and stored in a cool dark place. In this manner they keep at least 1 week, but links that have been cut must be used within several days. Canned lotus will keep 4 to 5 days (2 to 3 days in summer) stored in an airtight container with can liquid, and refrigerated. Amounts in recipes are for dry measure.

mirin
A sweet golden saké brewed only for cooking and used regularly in Japanese foods, *mirin* is a standard item at all Japanese food outlets, and recently, at some major supermarkets. The alcohol content usually runs from 12 to 14 percent, though some types have as little as 8 percent. *Mirin* has a distinctive and subtle flavor that cannot be approximated with a combination of ordinary saké and sugar. Since it is used as often as soy sauce and in small amounts in most instances, buy a bottle and keep it on hand. Once familiar with the properties of *mirin*, you may want to adjust amounts. Keeps 3 months after bottle has been opened.

miso (fermented soybean paste)

A basic staple in Japan, miso is used in soups, sauces, and dressed foods ("salads"), as a stuffing for trout (page 55), as a pickling agent for meat (page 70), as a flavoring agent, and so forth.

Because there are countless varieties of miso, numerous classification systems have arisen, causing much needless confusion for the Western consumer. For cooking purposes, miso can be divided according to salt content, which is either low (sweet), medium, or high. Sweet misos (low) work well in dressings, soups, and as a flavoring, and can be combined with misos that have a medium or high salt content for even greater variety; misos with medium salt content are good for general-purpose cooking, while misos high in salt add gusto to soups and other dishes.

There are no fast rules for using miso, so buy small amounts of several kinds and experiment, or consult your grocer. In general, the lighter the miso, the lower the salt content, but there are exceptions. If color or salt content is not specified in the recipe, any miso is fine. Look for miso in Japanese food markets, healthfood stores, and some supermarkets. Store in an airtight container or a sealed plastic bag. Sweet misos should be refrigerated, but saltier misos may be stored in a cool dark place. Misos keep up to 1 year, but since saltiness increases with age, sweet misos should be used fairly soon.

mustard, hot yellow (karashi)

Available in powdered form in small cans or as a ready-to-use paste in small tubes, this hot yellow mustard should be used sparingly, since a little goes a long way. Mix powdered mustard in the same manner as powdered *wasabi* horseradish (see page 33). Do not make it until needed, since flavor deteriorates quickly. Any hot mustard that is not sweet or vinegary makes an acceptable substitute. The ready-to-use mustard in a tube keeps 1 year refrigerated.

noodles

noodles—See cellophane noodles; *shirataki* filaments; *soba* noodles; *somen* noodles; *udon* noodles.

nori seaweed (nori)

Cultivated laver is dried to make this paper-thin seaweed product, which is high in iodine and vitamin A and low in calories. *Nori* seaweed comes in various sizes and grades. Buy full-sized sheets (approximately 7 × 8 inches/18 × 20 cm) of medium or high quality (the latter can be expensive), and, when making any of the rolled sushis (see pages 125–30), be especially careful to avoid low-quality products with patchy, nonuniform surfaces because they may break apart easily. The price is an additional clue to the quality.

Nori seaweed is almost always toasted before it is used in order to remove moisture, increase crispiness, and bring out flavor and fragrance. (Most *nori* sold today is pretoasted.) The one exception in this book is found in Tempura (page 138). Here untoasted *nori* seaweed (though pretoasted will certainly work) is dipped in batter and deep-fried, so toasting is unnecessary. To toast *nori* seaweed, pass the shiny side of the seaweed over an open gas flame several times until it crispens slightly and emits a fresh aroma like the seashore.

Since *nori* seaweed is quick to absorb moisture, store it in an airtight container and add a moisture-packet of desiccant, if possible. (These are often included with seaweed.) Seaweed may be refrigerated, if desired. Keeps 2 to 3 months.

Green *nori* seaweed (*ao-nori*), sold in flake (or powdered) form and one of the flavors in seven-spice mixture, is made from a different type of *nori* seaweed and has a different flavor. It is *not* a substitute for *nori* seaweed that is cut into shreds (or crumbled in dry cloth) and used as a garnish.

pickled plum (umeboshi)

This moist, fleshy salt-cured "plum" (a misnomer since it is actually an apricot) is thought to retard food spoilage, assist digestion, and sooth troubled stomachs, among other things. They are used here as one of the three fillings in Rice Balls (page 106). Pickled plums—available in bottles, plastic packs, or plastic tubs at Japanese markets—keep indefinitely refrigerated.

red pepper, dried (togarashi)

These red chili peppers, which are frequently used in abundance in other oriental cookery, are used sparingly in Japanese cooking. The seeds are extremely hot, so should generally be removed by soaking pepper in warm water, clipping off large end, and squeezing out seeds. Keep your fingers away from your eyes while handling peppers and be sure to wash your hands well when finished. Use any small dried red chili pepper sold in supermarkets or Chinese, Korean, and Japanese stores. Cayenne pepper is an acceptable substitute. Ground red pepper (*ichimi*) is also available at Japanese outlets. Store peppers in a closed cellophane or plastic bag.

rice
In Japanese cooking, short-grained rice—with its plump, pearly white or translucent grains—is cooked until tender and moist, and served daily by itself or combined with meat, fish, or vegetables. Cooking rice is a relatively simply procedure. For detailed explanations, see page 101. Instructions for preparing sushi rice are on page 121.

saké (rice wine)
Saké is used in small quantities in cooking but is not a substitute for *mirin*. (*Mirin*, a sweet saké brewed especially for cooking, is discussed in its own entry on page 28.) Besides its obvious flavor-enhancing qualities, saké also counteracts strong odors and covers excessive saltiness. Although saké is graded according to taste, aroma, and so on, there are fine sakés in the lowest class (*nikyu*, "second class") and mediocre sakés in the special class (*tokkyu*). Therefore, what tastes good as a drinking saké will work equally well as a seasoning.

Saké is stocked in many wine and liquor stores, and in the latter is most often found in the wine section. Large 1.9-quart (1.8-liter) bottles are the norm, but saké in quart (or liter) bottles and cartons is also available. The average alcohol content is 15 or 16 percent. Unopened, saké keeps 1 year. Check for a date on the bottle. Once opened, use within 1 or 2 months. Yellow-tinted sakés are perfectly fine, but if a saké has lost its crystal-clear transparency and become hazy or murky, it has gone bad.

sansho powder (kona-zansho)
This yellow-brown spice, made from the pod of the prickly ash, is tangy but mild. Suggested here as a seasoning for *Yakitori* (page 136), *sansho* powder is available at most Japanese provision outlets in small bottles or spice tins.

seaweed—See kelp, dried; *nori* seaweed; *wakame* seaweed.

sesame seeds (goma)
Freshly toasted and ground sesame seeds fill the kitchen with a delightful aroma and enhance the overall flavor of any dish. Since the reward is great in proportion to the effort and the difference is immediately noticeable, spend the few extra seconds it takes to toast sesame seeds and avoid commercial sesame paste (except in a pinch) along with pretoasted and ground sesame flakes (even in a pinch). Use white sesame seeds unless black is specifically called for, except in places where a black garnish would look more appealing. Store seeds in an airtight container and keep in a dry place.

Toasting and grinding: Since the oil in the seeds goes rancid after a while, taste seeds for freshness before using. Add seeds to a small dry frying pan and toast over a medium heat while stirring constantly and shaking pan. When seeds begin to make popping sounds, remove immediately from *pan*. (Seeds are easily overtoasted, since they are done before the color changes noticeably. If seeds are bitter, discard and prepare a new batch. After one or two practice runs, this simple technique will pose no problems.) Grind seeds using a small coffee grinder or a mortar and pestle. The final product should be rough, aromatic, and flaky. Make only as much as you need.

seven-spice mixture (shichimi or shichimi togarashi)
As the name implies, this multicolored

mixture is a blend of seven flavors: red pepper (*togarashi*), *sansho* (see *sansho* powder), sesame seeds or hemp seeds, poppy seeds, dried mandarin orange peel, perilla (*shiso*), and green *nori* seaweed (*ao-nori*; see *nori* seaweed). This mixture—sold in small spice tins, bottles, or plastic packets—is used to season *yakitori*, noodle dishes, some soups, and so on, as desired.

shiitake mushrooms (*Lentinus edodes*)

These brown mushrooms, sometimes referred to as "Chinese black mushrooms" or simply "Chinese mushrooms," are from 1½ to 4 inches (4 to 10 cm) in diameter and used not only in Japanese cooking, but Korean and Chinese as well. The dried version—which comes whole, sliced, crumpled, and even powdered—is readily available at most, if not all, oriental provision outlets.

Because dried *shiitake* mushrooms are more flavorful than fresh mushrooms (due to a natural chemical change during the drying process), they are generally preferred, are used to greater advantage in plain rice and sushi dishes, and can almost always be substituted for fresh *shiitake* with equally satisfactory or better results, except in such dishes as *Shabu-shabu* and Tempura, where fresh mushrooms are a must.

Good-quality dried mushrooms will emit a good, strong aroma and have full caps, a white underside, and thick flesh. If buying fresh *shiitake*, again look for thick-fleshed specimens with white undersides and choose only those with edges still tucked under (not spread). For both dried and fresh mushrooms, thicker is better and cracked caps, best (and expensive).

Soaking mushrooms: Dried mushrooms must be soaked in warm water until soft, which takes about 1 hour. Place a flat pan lid, drop-lid (see page 91), or any similar object on mushrooms to keep them submerged. Filling a bowl to the brim with water, adding mushrooms, and laying a plate (that has enough of a curve to keep mushrooms submerged) on top works just as well. Mushrooms soften quicker in warm water than in cold, and a drop-lid (or any acceptable substitute) not only keeps mushrooms immersed but also prevents water from cooling off, which would slow the softening process. Discard stems and use only caps. Soaking water makes a good stock. When in a hurry, substitute any fresh mushroom.

shirataki filaments ("white waterfall" filaments)

Made from the starch of the devils' tongue plant, these transparent, gelatinous filaments are best known as the "noodles" in Sukiyaki. Because of this, they are available at oriental food markets and some supermarkets. Look for them in cans on the shelf or in the refrigerated section sealed in plastic tubs or clear plastic packs filled with water. After opening, float filaments in pack liquid (add water if necessary) and refrigerate. Keeps 7 to 10 days. Unopened packs will keep at least 2 months refrigerated.

soba noodles (*soba*; buckwheat noodles)

These thin, buff-colored noodles, made with a combination of buckwheat and wheat flours, can be eaten hot or chilled. The best noodles are *hachiwari soba* (literally, "eighty-percent *soba*"), which call for one part wheat flour for every four parts buckwheat flour.

Dried noodles come loose or neatly banded together; fresh uncooked or cooked noodles (the latter only require several minutes of reheating; see step 4, page 109), if available, will be in the refrigerated section. A recipe for homemade *soba* noodles appears on page 108, and cooking instructions for both homemade and store-bought noodles are at the end of the recipe. (Cooking instructions are not always translated on packages.) Storage instructions are in the note following the recipe.

somen noodles (*somen*; "vermicelli")

These fine white noodles are made from wheat and have a diameter of less than one twenty-fifth of an inch (one millimeter). They come in different thicknesses and "flavors" (egg, green tea, *wakame* seaweed, and so on), though with the exception of egg *somen* the purpose is perhaps to offer additional colors for appearance' sake and the gift-giving seasons rather than to enhance the taste. Hand-stretched noodles (*tenobe somen*) are high quality and keep indefinitely. Machine-stretched products do not keep as well and should be eaten within a reasonable time. See page 114 for cooking instructions.

soy sauce (*shoyu*)

Many types of soy sauce are available, including synthetic ones, but these are best passed over in favor of naturally brewed soy sauce. Chinese soy sauce has a different body and affects foods differently, so use Japanese soy sauce for Japanese food. Low-salt soy sauce (*gen-en-shoyu*) that contains roughly 40 to 50 percent less salt is preferred by those concerned with salt intake. This is sometimes labeled as "lite," or "mild," soy sauce.

All recipes in this book call for "regular" dark soy sauce (*koi-kuchi shoyu*), the standard type sold in supermarkets. Light-colored soy sauce (*usu-kuchi shoyu*), which is amber-colored and saltier, is used for aesthetic reasons when its darker counterpart might darken the color of the dish. Refrigerate after opening or keep in a cool place.

tofu (*tofu*; bean curd)

Economical, versatile, and high in protein, tofu has finally received broad recognition in the United States as a healthy food. In addition to supplying necessary protein, tofu has no cholesterol and is low in carbohydrates.

All recipes call for regular, or "cotton," tofu (*momen tofu* or *dofu*), which is easily distinguished from the shiny- and slick-surfaced silk tofu (*kinu-goshi tofu* or *dofu*) by its rough, irregular exterior. Silk tofu has a softer and more delicate texture (and thus breaks apart easier during handling), and, although connoisseurs may argue, it can be substituted in places where tofu is cooked for short periods of time or at low temperatures. It is often used in clear soups. To store or to make homemade

tofu (regular), see page 79. "Instant homemade tofu" products are also available in a powdered form.

Freeze-dried tofu (*kori-dofu, Koya-dofu,* or *shimi-dofu*) contains much protein and has an advantage over the other tofu products listed here because it keeps 3 to 4 months. It has a delightful texture and absorbs flavors well. Cakes are small, lightweight, and beige. To reconstitute, see page 85, step 1. Freeze-dried tofu cannot be used as a replacement for fresh tofu.

Okara (tofu pulp), a byproduct of tofu making, is left over when the soy milk to be coagulated is strained (see Homemade Tofu, page 80, step 5). Although it has little flavor of its own, *okara* is quick to absorb other flavors. Keeps 1 day refrigerated and 1 month frozen. Sautéed (see page 86, step 3) or oven-roasted *okara* keeps 5 to 7 days. (See also *Okara* and Vegetable Mélange, page 86.)

Thick deep-fried tofu (*atsuage* or *namaage*) comes in rectangles, squares, and triangles all approximately 1 inch (2½ cm) thick. Deep-fried at a high temperature, *atsuage* has a spongy golden exterior and a soft white interior. Rinse with boiling water and pat dry with towels before using. It may be added to miso soups and simmered dishes. Keeps 4 to 5 days at most, refrigerated in a plastic bag. *Atsuage* keeps well frozen.

Thin deep-fried tofu (*aburage* or *usuage*) is deep-fried twice after the tofu has been sliced into thin sheets and pressed to remove excess water. Because of this process and because a tofu made especially for making *aburage* is utilized, *aburage* cannot be made at home. Fresh *aburage* is a light golden color and soft and puffy. High-quality products have thick edges and are slightly concave at the center. Old specimens are dark and have stiff (not soft) edges. Rinse well with boiling water and pat dry before using. As with *atsuage*, keeps 4 to 5 days at most, refrigerated in a plastic bag and keeps well frozen.

udon noodles (*udon*)

Outside Japan these thick, round (sometimes flat) noodles are most often found in their dried form. Since they are a basic flour-and-water noodle, fresh uncooked or fresh cooked noodles (the latter only require several minutes of reheating; see step 4, page 109) may also be available in some areas.

After cooking, noodles are rinsed to remove starch and then reheated to serve. Noodles should be served *al dente*—tender inside and out but slightly firm at the center. A recipe for homemade *udon* noodles appears on page 108, and cooking instructions for both homemade and storebought noodles are at the end of the recipe. (Cooking instructions are not always translated on packages.) Storage instructions are in the note following the recipe.

vinegar, rice (*kome su*)

All recipes call for rice vinegar rather than a heavier fruit or wine vinegar, with the exception of Beef Tatare (page 69), which calls for wine vinegar. Available at many of the larger supermarkets, not to mention Chinese and Japanese stores. Its lightness is essential for seasoning sushi rice and advisable for vinegared "salads" and so on. Cider vinegar makes the best substitute. Once opened, rice vinegar keeps 1 year.

wakame seaweed (*wakame*)

Delicious in soups and salads alike, *wakame* is thought to strengthen hair and give it a healthy luster. Before using dried *wakame*, soften it by soaking it in water for 10 minutes. Do not leave *wakame* in water too long. Remove the tough central spine if it was not removed during processing. *Wakame* loses much of its nutritional value if cooked more than 1 minute, so add to soups just before serving. Keeps at least 3 months stored in an airtight container and refrigerated.

wasabi horseradish (*wasabi*)

This green horseradish gives sushi its extra bite and is used as a condiment in tandem with soy sauce as a dip for sashimi. Because the cultivation of Japanese horseradish requires fresh cold mountain water and is time-consuming, fresh *wasabi* root has become a luxury in Japan, and most households use ready-to-use pastes (in tubes) or powders (in small tins), both reasonable substitutes.

Powdered *wasabi* horseradish is easily reconstituted: combine with a small amount of warm water and mix until a smooth, thick paste is formed, then cover and set aside for 10 minutes to allow flavor to mature. Make only as much as is necessary and use it sparingly. Dry powdered *wasabi* keeps indefinitely, but once mixed it should be used the same day. The small ready-to-use pastes keep 1 year refrigerated. For decorative devices, see CUCUMBER CUP (page 49) and WASABI HORSERADISH CONE on page 52.

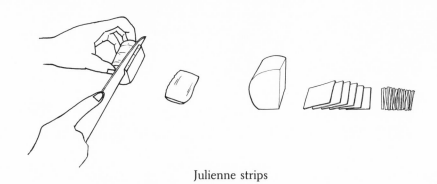

Julienne strips

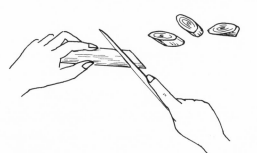

Diagonal slices

Slivers

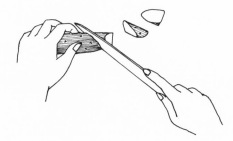

Wedges and chunks

SOUPS

Primary Bonito Stock
(Ichiban dashi)

Primary bonito stock is used in all clear soups and can be used in dishes that call for a particularly subtle stock. Originally made with fresh shavings from bonito fillets that had been dried outside in the shade, most Japanese households today prepare stock using packaged flakes. Many cooks now go one step further and substitute the time-saving instant liquids or powders such as those discussed in the note below.

MAKES 3½ TO 4 CUPS

4-inch (10-cm) piece kelp (*konbu*)
4 cups cold water
1½–2 cups (loose) fresh bonito
  flakes or packaged flakes (called
  either *hana-katsuo* or *kezuri-bushi*)

•1. Do not wash kelp, since the white powder on the surface contains much of the flavor of the kelp. Instead, lightly wipe both sides of kelp with a damp cloth and make ½-inch (1½-cm) cuts with scissors at 1-inch (2½-cm) intervals to release flavor.

•2. Add cold water to medium-sized saucepan. When water is bath-water warm (100°F/38°C), add kelp. Cook, uncovered, over medium heat and remove kelp just *before* water boils.

•3. Add bonito flakes to kelp broth and raise heat to medium-high. When broth begins to boil, remove pan from heat immediately. Skim off any foam.

•4. Allow 2 or 3 minutes for flakes to settle to bottom, then slowly pour stock through cheesecloth-lined strainer, making sure no flakes get into stock. (Bonito flakes will destroy the stock's delicacy.) *Do not squeeze cheesecloth.* The stock should be clear. Use as necessary. Reserve kelp and bonito flakes for making Secondary Bonito Stock (see following recipe).

NOTE: Many instant bonito stock, or instant *dashi*, products are available for quick preparation of primary or secondary bonito stock. Instant bonito stock, which comes in granule or liquid form and contains bonito and kelp flavoring, is an acceptable substitute. Bonito extract (*katsuo-dashi*) can be used in place of bonito flakes, and kelp extract (*konbu-dashi*) in place of kelp. All instant products can be used to make primary or secondary stock.

Secondary Bonito Stock
(Niban dashi)

Secondary bonito stock is used in many simmered and one-pot dishes, miso soups, vegetable dishes, and so on. Using flakes and kelp left over from primary bonito stock is perfectly fine and economical. Stored in a sealed bottle and refrigerated, it will keep up to 3 days. See also note in preceding recipe.

MAKES 2 TO 2½ CUPS	MAKES 4 TO 4½ CUPS
2½ cups cold water	4½ cups cold water
bonito flakes reserved from primary bonito stock	2 cups loose bonito flakes (*hana-katsuo*)
kelp reserved from primary bonito stock	3-inch (8-cm) piece kelp (*konbu*)

•1. In a small saucepan, combine water, bonito flakes, and kelp (lightly wipe with damp cloth and make ½-inch [1½-cm] cuts with scissors at 1-inch [2½-cm] intervals as in Primary Bonito Stock if using a new piece of kelp).

•2. Bring to a soft boil over a medium heat and cook, uncovered, for 4 or 5 minutes.

•3. Filter through cheesecloth-lined strainer. Squeeze cheesecloth to release remaining liquid. Use as necessary.

Egg-drop Soup
(Kakitama-jiru)

A favorite with young and old alike, this soup goes well with any meal and can be served year round. The egg—suspended in sparkling clear broth—floats in the soup as lightly as clouds drift across the sky. It takes almost no practice to master this popular dish.

SERVES 4	79 Cal. per serving

2 eggs
1 Tbsp saké
3½ cups primary bonito stock
1⅓ tsps salt
1 tsp soy sauce
1 Tbsp cornstarch
1 rounded Tbsp finely chopped green onion tops
4 tiny pieces lemon or lime zest (optional)

•1. Combine eggs, saké, and a pinch salt. Beat, frothing as little as possible.

•2. Bring bonito stock to a boil over medium heat. Add salt and soy sauce, then reduce to simmer.

•3. Mix cornstarch with 2 Tbsps water, then blend evenly into soup, stirring constantly.

•4. While beating egg mixture continuously, pour into soup in a fine stream. *Do not stir soup.* When final egg threads have set, remove from heat.

•5. Serve in preheated soup bowls (see following note). Garnish each bowl with finely chopped green onions and sliver of zest.

NOTE: Clear and miso soups are best when served as hot as possible in small, deep soup bowls. In cold weather, preheating soup bowls is desirable. To do this, fill bowls with hot water and let stand 1 or 2 minutes. Empty and dry bowls, then pour in hot soup and serve.

Somen and Cucumber Soup
(Somen to kyuri no suimono)

This soup's appeal is its simplicity—crisp cucumber slices float at the surface while a few tender noodles nestled together at the bottom of the bowl beckon. An excellent summer soup.

SERVES 4	41 Cal. per serving

16 *somen* noodles, about ½ oz (15 g)
¼ cucumber
3½ cups primary bonito stock
1 tsp salt
1 tsp soy sauce

•1. Cook noodles following package directions or instructions on page 114.

•2. Peel and seed cucumber. Cut crosswise into thin slices.

•3. Bring bonito stock to a boil. Add salt and soy sauce. While stock is heating, preheat soup bowls (see above note), place cooked noodles in bottom of bowl, and distribute cucumber rounds on top. Add hot stock and serve.

Clear Soup with Chicken and Okra
(Tori to okura no suimono)

Juicy bite-sized chunks of chicken and thin slices of crisp okra added just before serving offer contrasting textures in this uncomplicated soup. Select okra that is young, tender (not stringy), and unblemished.

4 oz (115 g) chicken breast fillet
   without skin
2 tsps saké
2 Tbsps cornstarch
4 whole okra
3½ cups primary bonito stock
1 tsp soy sauce
1 tsp salt

•1. Cut chicken diagonally into bite-sized pieces. Sprinkle with a pinch salt and 1 tsp saké. Coat chicken with cornstarch. Cook in boiling water until it floats to top (3–4 minutes). Remove and cool in pan of cold water. Drain.

•2. Cut "caps" off okra and slice into rounds.

•3. Bring bonito stock to a boil. Add okra, soy sauce, 1 tsp salt, and 1 tsp saké. Remove from heat. Preheat soup bowls (see note on page 37), place chicken in bowls, and add soup and sliced okra.

Shrimp and Asparagus Soup
(Ebi shinjo to asuparagasu no suimono)

The delicate pink of the cooked shrimp and the sober green of the tender asparagus please the eye as well as the palate and give this soup the simple poetic elegance that clear soups are known for. A wonderful meal-opener when entertaining.

5 oz (140 g) raw shrimp or prawns
1 egg white
1 Tbsp cornstarch
1¼ tsps salt
4 stalks fresh asparagus
1 tsp *mirin*
3½ cups primary bonito stock
1 tsp soy sauce
1 tsp fresh ginger juice (optional; see
   page 27)

To prepare
•1. Shell shrimp, then devein by inserting a toothpick at the curve of the back and pulling out the alimentary canal. Remove tails. Place shells in a small saucepan with ¾ cup water and boil over medium heat until water is reduced by half. Strain this broth through cheesecloth. Discard shells.

•2. Purée shrimp in food processor or blender (or by using a mortar and pestle).

•3. Add egg white, cornstarch, 3 Tbsps shrimp broth, and ¼ tsp salt to shrimp and blend.

To cook and serve

•1. Cut asparagus into thirds and discard the tough lower third. To 3 cups boiling water add pinch salt and asparagus. Cook 2 or 3 minutes until tender-crisp. Drain and sprinkle with *mirin* and pinch salt.

•2. Bring bonito stock to a boil. With a spoon, gently slip a portion of shrimp into boiling stock. When shrimp "quenelles" rise to the surface, rotate until they sink slightly and continue to boil until they once more surface and have turned a delicate pink (about 2 minutes).

•3. Add soy sauce and 1 tsp salt. Remove from heat and add ginger juice. Preheat soup bowls (see note on page 37). Add 2 pieces asparagus and 1 shrimp quenelle to each bowl. Divide soup among bowls and serve.

Miso Soup with Tofu and *Wakame* Seaweed
(Tofu to wakame no miso-shiru)

Protein-rich miso soups have endless possibilities because of the numerous types of miso available. Tofu, miso, and wakame *seaweed is a highly nourishing combination. This delicate seaweed is widely used in Japanese soups and salads, has no calories, and is thought to be high in the minerals that give hair a healthy sheen.*

SERVES 4	120 Cal. per serving

1–2 oz (30–60 g) dried *wakame*
   seaweed
1 cake regular tofu, about 10 oz (285 g)
3½ cups secondary bonito stock
4 Tbsps medium-salt miso
1 rounded Tbsp finely chopped green
   onion tops

•1. Soak *wakame* seaweed until it softens (about 10 minutes). Do not oversoak. Drain and trim away any tough sections, then cut into 1-inch (2½ -cm) lengths. Cut tofu into ½ -inch (1½ -cm) cubes.

•2. Heat bonito stock over medium flame. When lukewarm, extract ½ cup stock and blend in miso, making sure there are no lumps. Slowly blend mixture back into stock. Continue to heat *but do not boil.*

•3. When miso is completely dissolved, add tofu and *wakame* seaweed. Remove from heat just *before* soup boils.

•4. Divide among preheated soup bowls (see note on page 37). Garnish with green onions.

NOTE: All miso soups separate easily when left standing. The miso is heavier and falls to the bottom while the bonito stock remains on the top. Just before taking a sip, stir the soup once or twice with your spoon. If it is necessary to reheat miso soup, do not allow it to boil.

Miso Soup with Potato and Leek
(Jagaimo to negi no miso-shiru)

In choosing the ingredients for miso soups, it is best to pick one that sinks and one that floats, and potato and leek is just such a combination. Use a low-salt red miso, if possible. In general, the lighter the miso, the lower the salt content; but there are exceptions.

SERVES 4	80 Cal. per serving

½ lb (225 g) potatoes
3 leeks
4 cups secondary bonito stock
4 Tbsps low-salt miso

•1. Peel potatoes. Slice into quarters lengthwise, then crosswise into ½-inch (1½-cm) slices. Rinse starch from potatoes in a bowl of cold water. Drain.

•2. Cut leeks into 1-inch (2½-cm) lengths.

•3. Cook potatoes in stock over medium-high heat. When potatoes are half done, add leeks. Cook until vegetables are tender. Skim off foam.

•4. When potatoes and leeks are done, extract ½ cup stock and blend with miso, making sure there are no lumps. Slowly blend miso mixture back into stock. Remove from heat just *before* soup boils.

•5. Preheat soup bowls (see note on page 37) and ladle in soup and vegetables.

Miso Soup with Mixed Vegetables
(Miso kenchin-jiru)

Known as miso-kenchin *because of the tofu-and-vegetable combination, this dish has something for everybody. It is rich in vitamins and protein and is a wise choice on a cold winter evening. Substitute seasonal vegetables.*

SERVES 4	215 Cal. per serving

4 dried *shiitake* mushrooms
5 inches (13 cm) burdock, about 2 oz
    (60 g) (if available)
2 inches (5 cm) daikon radish or 3 oz
    (85 g) white radish or turnip
4 inches (10 cm) carrot
1 medium potato
1 cake regular tofu, about 10 oz (285 g)
2 Tbsps vegetable oil
3½ cups secondary bonito stock
4–5 Tbsps miso
1 rounded Tbsp finely chopped green
    onion tops

To prepare

•**1.** Soak mushrooms in warm water until soft (about 1 hour), keeping them submerged by covering with drop-lid (see page 91), flat pan lid, or saucer. Discard stems and cut caps into quarters lengthwise. If using large mushrooms, slice into ½-inch (1½-cm) wide strips.

•**2.** Scrub burdock well with a stiff brush under running water but do not scrape or peel. Rotate root while whittling into thin slivers, as if sharpening a pencil. Soak burdock in water until ready to use.

•**3.** Peel daikon and carrot. Slice into rectangular strips 1½ × ½ × ⅛ inches (4 × 1½ × ½ cm).

•**4.** Peel potato. Cut into ½-inch (1½-cm) cubes. Rinse starch from potato in a bowl of cold water. Drain.

•**5.** Add whole tofu to boiling water and boil for 1 minute, turning once. Drain and cool. Wrap in cheesecloth, twist ends, and gently squeeze out excess moisture. Turn out into colander and crumble into small pieces.

To cook and serve

•**1.** Preheat a large, deep skillet and add oil. Stir-fry burdock for 1 minute. Add daikon and carrot. Cook, stirring constantly, for 1 minute. At 30-second intervals add mushroom, potato, and tofu.

•**2.** Pour in bonito stock and skim off any foam. Cover and bring quickly to a boil. Reduce to simmer and cook, uncovered, until vegetables are tender (10–15 minutes). Skim off foam occasionally.

•**3.** Remove ½ cup bonito stock and blend with miso, making sure there are no lumps. Slowly blend miso mixture back into vegetable broth.

•**4.** Serve in preheated soup bowls (see note on page 37) garnished with finely chopped green onions.

Smoked Salmon and Daikon Rolls
(Sake no daikon maki)

Smoked salmon rolled in clean white strips of daikon radish and marinated in sweet vinegar is an impressive prelude to any meal. This hors d'oeuvre involves little actual preparation and makes simplicity look sophisticated. Since it easily keeps 1 week refrigerated (soaking in sweet vinegar), it is perfect for parties. Make it ahead of time, and set one worry aside.

MAKES 8–10 PIECES	37 Cal. per piece

4 oz (225 g) smoked salmon, thinly sliced
3 inches (8 cm) daikon radish
1 ½ tsps salt
toothpicks

SWEET VINEGAR
4 Tbsps rice vinegar
3 Tbsps sugar

•1. Peel daikon. Cut in half lengthwise and thinly slice into at least 16 sheets, each roughly 2 × 3 inches (5 × 8 cm). Soak in 2 ½ cups cold water with 1 ½ tsps salt until soft and pliable (about 15 minutes).

•2. Lay out 3 or 4 pieces of daikon in a row, with each overlapping the previous piece slightly, cover with salmon slices, roll, and secure with toothpick. Soak in SWEET VINEGAR for 2 hours or until ready to serve, whichever is longer.

•3. Remove toothpick and cut rolls in half crosswise, stand cut side facing up, and serve. Secure with a new toothpick, if desired.

1

2

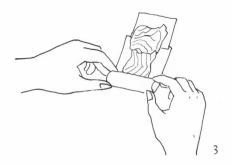
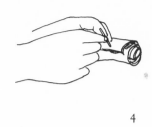

3

4

Skewered Chicken Quenelles
(Tori tsukune yaki to kyuri no kushizashi)

MAKES APPROX. 12 SKEWERS   45 Cal. per skewer

½ lb (225 g) ground chicken
1 Tbsp oil
1 cucumber
salt
bamboo skewers (see page 137) or 6-
    to 8-inch (15- to 20-cm) metal
    skewers

INGREDIENTS A	INGREDIENTS B
2 tsps soy sauce	1 egg white
2 tsps saké	1½ Tbsps cornstarch
2 tsps sugar	2 tsps sugar
1 tsp fresh ginger juice (see page 27)	1 tsp soy sauce

•1. Divide chicken in half and set one portion aside. Combine other half with INGREDIENTS A in a saucepan. Sauté over medium heat, stirring constantly, until chicken has lost its pink color (1–2 minutes). Place saucepan in shallow pan of ice water and force-cool chicken by stirring mixture until it reaches room temperature.

•2. In a food processor (or blender) combine cooked chicken, remaining uncooked chicken, and INGREDIENTS B. Process until mixture is a smooth paste (6–8 seconds; slightly longer, if using blender). If consistency of mixture is not firm enough to hold a ball shape, mix in a little more cornstarch.

•3. Heat oil in a preheated skillet over low heat. Drop in chicken by rounded tsp and cook until browned (about 5 minutes on each side). Finished quenelles should be firm on the outside and soft inside. Remove from skillet.

•4. Peel and seed cucumber. Quarter lengthwise and cut into bite-sized pieces. Skewer chicken and cucumber alternately, 1 or 2 pieces of each on a skewer. Serve hot or at room temperature.

Chicken-stuffed Squash Balls
(Kabocha to tori no kushizashi)

Deep-fried squash balls stuffed with sautéed chicken and garnished with carved radishes are a provocative and memorable hors d'oeuvre. Crisp, bite-sized pieces of cucumber can be substituted for radishes.

MAKES 8 SKEWERS	73 Cal. per skewer

2 oz (60 g) ground chicken
1 tsp soy sauce
1 tsp saké
7 oz (200 g) winter squash (orange or yellow flesh)
2 Tbsps sugar
2 Tbsps cornstarch
2 cups vegetable oil for deep-frying
8 bamboo skewers (see page 137)

RADISH ROSE
8 small red radishes
2 Tbsps rice vinegar
1½ Tbsps sugar

•1. Begin preparing RADISH ROSE (see facing page).

•2. In a saucepan mix ground chicken with soy sauce and saké. Sauté over low heat, stirring constantly, until chicken loses its pink color. Cool. Divide into 8 equal portions.

•3. Cut squash into chunks, then peel. Combine in saucepan with sugar and enough water to barely cover. Cook, uncovered, until squash is tender. Drain. Mash, then divide into 8 equal portions.

•4. On a 8-inch (20-cm) square of plastic wrap held in one palm, spread 1 portion squash into a circle 3 inches (8 cm) in diameter. Place 1 portion chicken in center of squash. Bring up ends of plastic wrap to enclose chicken in squash. Twist ends of plastic to form squash into a ball (see page 120).

•5. Roll squash balls in cornstarch. Heat oil to high deep-frying temperature (360°F/180°C) and deep-fry. Drain on absorbent paper.

•6. Drain radishes. Thread 1 squash ball and 1 radish on each skewer. Serve hot or at room temperature.

Soft Simmered Chicken Gizzards
(Sunagimo no yawaraka-ni)

This easily prepared dish has a special appeal for dieters looking for a highly nutritious and low-calorie hors d'oeuvre. A quick no-fuss appetizer.

10 whole chicken gizzards
1 leek
4 Tbsps soy sauce
¾ cup saké
2 tsps hot yellow Japanese mustard
   (*karashi*) or any yellow mustard that
   is not sweet or vinegary
toothpicks

•1. Prepare using one of the following two methods.

Pressure cooker method: Cut leek into 2-inch (5-cm) pieces and crush with the side of a knife. Combine all ingredients except mustard in pressure cooker with ¾ cup water. Secure lid, bring to full pressure, and simmer for 30 minutes.

Saucepan method: Prepare leek in same manner. Combine all ingredients except mustard in a saucepan with 4 cups water. Cover and simmer over medium heat for 1½ hours.

•2. When gizzards are cool enough to handle (discard leek), cut in half. Skewer 2 pieces on a toothpick. Dab a little mustard on each portion and serve.

Radish Rose

These easy-to-make carved radishes with their red-rimmed "rose petals" make an elegant garnish. Begin preparing radishes at least an hour before you need them. Radishes keep 2 days refrigerated in a bowl of sweet vinegar. After that they will gradually lose their color. See cover photograph and color plate (page 18).

8 small red radishes
2 Tbsps rice vinegar
1½ Tbsps sugar

1. Trim radishes. Make a slight cut in surface of radish to form "petal." Cut away center portion of petal to expose white flesh. Continue around radish in layers to the top. Soak in water to allow petals to separate and to remove some of the sharp flavor (10–20 minutes).

2. Sprinkle radishes lightly with salt and set aside until radishes soften slightly (about 10 minutes). Rinse in cold water. Soak in rice vinegar and sugar (sweet vinegar) for 30 minutes or until ready to use, whichever is longer.

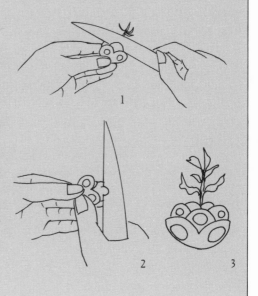

Pork and Vegetable Kebabs
(Kushi katsu)

This appetizer—with larger portions than most—will temporarily appease voracious appetites, so it is especially useful when a long interval is anticipated between hors d'oeuvres and dinner. Kebabs can be attractively served by inserting bases of skewers into the rounded side of a cabbage half. Increase the amount of pork and size of cubes and these kebabs can be served as a main dish.

MAKES 8 SKEWERS   156 Cal. per skewer
---

5 oz (140 g) pork loin
2 inches (5 cm) small eggplant
½ bell pepper
1 leek or ½ bulb onion
salt and pepper
2–3 cups vegetable oil for deep-frying
1 orange or lemon, sliced (optional garnish)
8 bamboo skewers (see page 137)

SAUCE
3 Tbsps Worcestershire sauce
3 Tbsps ketchup
1 Tbsp soy sauce

BREADING
2 Tbsps flour
1 egg and 1 Tbsp water
1 cup fine dried bread crumbs

•1. Slice eggplant into ½-inch (1½-cm) rounds and soak in cold water for 5 minutes. Pat dry with paper towel. Cut bell pepper into 4 pieces, leek into 1-inch (2½-cm) lengths (or quarter onion), and pork into 8 bite-sized pieces.

•2. Mix SAUCE ingredients.

•3. Make 4 skewers of pork and eggplant, and 4 skewers of pork, bell pepper, and leek. (Skewered foods should be touching.)

•4. Lay out BREADING ingredients. Sprinkle skewers with salt and pepper. Coat skewered foods with flour, egg-and-water mixture, and bread crumbs in that order.

•5. Heat oil in a wok or skillet to medium deep-frying temperature (340°F/170°C). Deep-fry 4 skewers at one time, turning once, until pork is cooked and skewers are browned on both sides. Drain on absorbent paper.

•6. If desired, wrap skewer ends in foil for easier handling when serving. Garnish serving platter with orange (or lemon) slices and serve with sauce as a dip (or pour over skewered food).

Shrimp Sushi

(Ebi no kimi-zushi)

Lightly vinegared scrambled egg replaces the traditional sushi rice in this attractive red and yellow appetizer. Good finger food.

MAKES 8 PIECES   78 Cal. per piece

8 shrimp, about 2½ inches (6½ cm)
  without head
8 toothpicks
4½ Tbsps rice vinegar
3½–4 Tbsps sugar
3 eggs
1 egg yolk
⅛ tsp salt

•1. *Shrimp*: Shell and devein shrimp (see page 38), leaving tail and shell segment closest to tail intact. Straighten shrimp by inserting a toothpick through the length of shrimp from tail end. Place in a saucepan, sprinkle with salt, and barely cover with water. Boil until shrimp turn pink (2–3 minutes). Drain. Remove toothpicks. Cut underside of shrimp lengthwise from tip to tail, so that 2 halves of shrimp fan out and lay flat. Soak in 3 Tbsps rice vinegar mixed with 2 to 2½ Tbsps sugar for about 10 minutes.

•2. *Egg*: In a saucepan combine eggs, egg yolk, ⅛ tsp salt, and 1½ Tbsps sugar. Stir constantly over medium-high heat until egg is soft scrambled. Add 1½ Tbsps rice vinegar and continue cooking and stirring until egg is firmly cooked but not hard. Remove from heat. Force through a fine sieve or whir in food processor (or blender) until it reaches a smooth consistency (3–4 seconds; slightly longer, if using blender).

•3. Divide egg into 8 portions. To shape, place 1 portion in your hand and squeeze gently by closing your hand shut. Smooth any rough edges with index and middle fingers of other hand, while holding egg in cupped hand. Place shrimp on egg, cut side down.

•4. Serve 2 pieces sushi per person on small dessert plates or arrange all pieces on a single plate radiating out from the center with tails pointing outward.

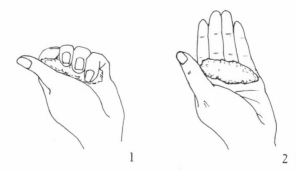

1   2

FISH

Sashimi

Sashimi's growing popularity outside Japan attests to its intrinsic appeal. This recipe offers guidelines for preparing sashimi to be served as a side dish during the normal course of a meal. Ultimate freshness is a must; if there is any doubt about the freshness of the seafood, do not use it. Fish frozen soon after it has been caught to preserve it in the freshest state possible has made sashimi a feasible dish even in noncoastal areas. If you live near a coast, choose fresh local seafood rather than the frozen specimens, since freshness and taste will be far superior. Consult your fishmonger for sashimi-quality fish in season.

Sashimi is usually served early in the meal so that its subtle flavor can be appreciated before stronger foods affect the palate. Garnishes and condiments aid in digestion, refresh the palate, and bring out the natural flavor of the fish. (See also Sashimi Platter Supreme, page 51.)

SERVES 4	218 Cal. per serving

½ lb (225 g) fresh or frozen raw tuna fillet, approximately 8 × 2 × 1 inches (20 × 5 × 2½ cm)

4 oz (115 g) fresh or frozen raw squid

CONDIMENTS
1 tsp *wasabi* horseradish
soy sauce

GARNISHES
¾ cucumber
1 cup shredded daikon radish or white radish
4 small sprigs chervil or any delicate herb (optional; perilla [*shiso*] leaves are traditional)

To prepare

•1. Prepare cucumber cups (see facing page) now or *wasabi* horseradish cones (see page 52) just before serving, keeping in mind that powdered *wasabi* needs 10 minutes to mature.

•2. Prepare GARNISHES. Peel daikon. Peel and seed remaining cucumber. Shred both. These will be a decorative bed for sashimi. Soak separately in cold water until ready to use.

•3. *To cut tuna*: Clean cutting board well before slicing sashimi. Using a very sharp knife and slicing crosswise, cut tuna into ⅜-inch (1-cm) thick pieces by pulling the knife toward you in one long, continuous motion while applying a slight downward pressure (see following page).

•4. *Squid*: Reach into cavity above head and detach head from body with fingers (see next page). Pull away head and legs. (Reserve legs for other uses.) Take out and discard transparent cartilage from body cavity. Insert finger under tail flaps and disengage, then pull off tail flaps. (Some skin will come away when you do this.) Peel away remaining skin. If skin is difficult to peel, rub with salt or cheesecloth. Slit body open lengthwise and wash. Score dull inside surface at ¼-inch (¾-cm) intervals in a diamond pattern. Turn squid over so that shiny outside faces up. Cut in half lengthwise, then crosswise into ½-inch (1-cm) wide strips.

To assemble and serve

•1. For individual servings, use shallow decorative bowls. Drain garnishes and squeeze out excess water by hand. Make a mound of shredded daikon and cucumber at the back edge of the bowl. Lean a sprig of herb against daikon and cucumber, then place several slices of tuna up against (or on top of) shredded vegetables. Slide knife under 4 or 5 squid slices, lift, and place alongside tuna, tucking under edges.

•2. Place a small amount of *wasabi* in the cucumber cup (or make *wasabi* horseradish cone). Attractively place this alongside sashimi. Provide small dipping dishes of soy sauce for each person. Sashimi is dipped in soy sauce spiced with *wasabi* to taste.

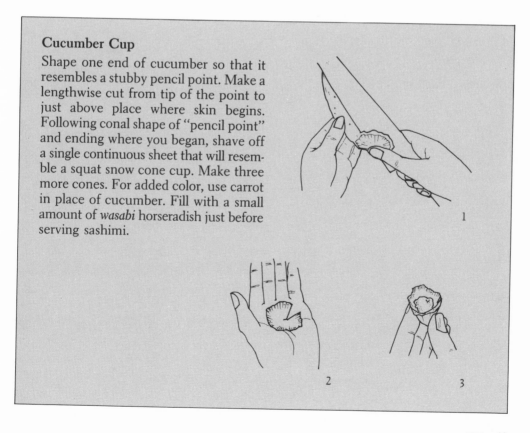

Cucumber Cup

Shape one end of cucumber so that it resembles a stubby pencil point. Make a lengthwise cut from tip of the point to just above place where skin begins. Following conal shape of "pencil point" and ending where you began, shave off a single continuous sheet that will resemble a squat snow cone cup. Make three more cones. For added color, use carrot in place of cucumber. Fill with a small amount of *wasabi* horseradish just before serving sashimi.

Cutting tuna sashimi

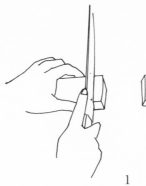

1

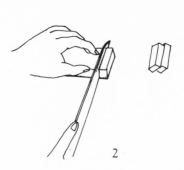

2

Cleaning and cutting squid

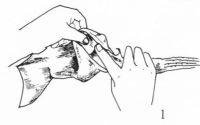

1

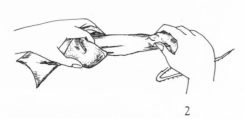

2

3

4

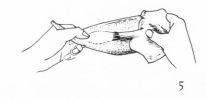

5

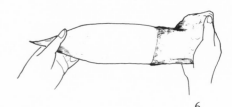

6

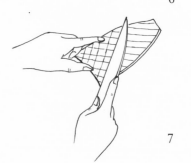

7

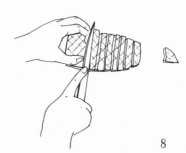

8

Sashimi Platter Supreme

Additional suggestions and arrangements are offered here. Again, choose only the freshest sashimi-quality fish and shellfish. Do this and you cannot fail. An array of sparkling fresh seafood thoughtfully arranged is an impressive sight. Follow the easy instructions below to make the sashimi rose and amaze yourself and guests. Hot saké is an excellent accompaniment.

SERVES 6–8   198 Cal. per serving

½ lb (225 g) fresh or frozen raw
 tuna fillet, approximately
 8 × 2 × 1 inches (20 × 5 × 2½ cm)
1 sheet *nori* seaweed, toasted
4 oz (115 g) fresh or frozen raw
 squid
5 very fresh horse mackerel or
 equivalent amount of any
 sashimi-quality fish
4 very fresh large scallops
4 oz (115 g) very fresh sole or sea
 bream or red snapper fillet

GARNISHES
1 cup shredded daikon radish or
 white radish
1 cucumber
4 small sprigs chervil or any
 delicate herb (optional; perilla
 [*shiso*] leaves are traditional)

CONDIMENTS
wasabi horseradish
soy sauce

•**1.** Make cucumber cup (see page 49) now or *wasabi* horseradish cone (see next page) just before serving, keeping in mind that powdered *wasabi* horseradish needs 10 minutes to mature.

•**2.** Prepare GARNISHES. Peel daikon and shred. Peel, seed, and shred remaining cucumber. Shredded vegetables will be a decorative bed for sashimi. Soak separately in cold water until ready to use.

•**3.** Make sashimi rose, if desired (see following page).

•**4.** Prepare sashimi.

Tuna and tuna rolls: From tuna fillet cut a lengthwise strip about ½ inch (1 cm) wide. Cut strip in half lengthwise so that you have 2 strips about 8 inches (20 cm) long and ½ inch (1 cm) square. Cut *nori* seaweed in half lengthwise. If *nori* has not been pretoasted, toast by lightly passing shiny side over an open flame several times. Rub tuna with *wasabi* horseradish and soy sauce to taste, and wrap in *nori*. Cut into 1-inch (2½-cm) pieces. (If preparing sashimi far in advance, reserve strips of tuna, and roll just before serving sashimi.) Cut remaining tuna into ⅜-inch (1-cm) thick slices (for cutting technique, see previous recipe).

Squid: Clean (instructions in preceding recipe). Cut crosswise into ½-inch (1-cm) wide strips.

Horse mackerel: Remove head, tail, bones, and entrails. Remove fine bones with tweezers. Salt skin and then peel off. Cut into bite-sized pieces.

Scallops: Wash in 3 cups water and 2½ tsps salt. Slice into thin rounds.

Sole and other fish fillets: Cut into ½-inch (1-cm) wide slices.

•**5.** Drain shredded cucumber and daikon, then squeeze out excess moisture by hand. Make several small mounds of each and nestle sprig of herb and slices of sashimi up against each mound. Stand pieces of tuna roll on end (hide uneven ends) and place on platter. Add remaining sashimi. See color plate (page 8) for a decorative arrangement.

•6. Place a small amount of *wasabi* in cucumber cups (or make large *wasabi* horseradish cones). Attractively arrange on serving platter. Provide small dipping dishes of soy sauce for each person. Dip sashimi into soy sauce spiced with *wasabi* to taste.

Sashimi Rose

This impressive decoration is easy to make. Slice thin pieces from tuna fillet at 45° angle. Loosely roll up one slice and stand it on end in the center of serving platter so that the more ragged of the two edges (originally part of top or bottom of fillet) becomes the lips of petals. Wrap around other slices until flower is desired size. Bend back petal edges so that flower "blooms." Place a dab of *wasabi* in center. If desired, decorate with leaves from a rose bush. Alternating red (tuna) and white (thinly sliced squid) petals is an interesting variation.

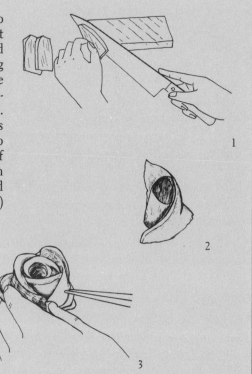

Wasabi Horseradish Cone

Powdered *wasabi* (not ready-to-use paste) can be decoratively shaped, once it has been mixed and allowed to mature. Mix *wasabi* 15 to 20 minutes before serving sashimi, following instructions on container (or see page 33). After mix has matured (about 10 minutes), form into cone with thumb, index, and middle fingers. Place one small cone in each dish. (For Sashimi Platter Supreme, make larger cones.)

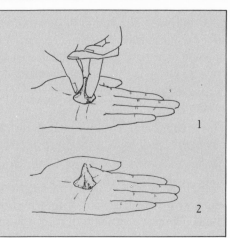

Quick-seared Bonito Sashimi
(Katsuo no tataki)

This sashimi has the flavor of ginger, daikon radish, and green onions throughout. Because the flavor is subtle, it must be served at the beginning of the meal, when the palate is clear. The Japanese name—which means to pat, or "beat," in the flavor—is derived from the technique found in step 4. This recipe calls for a lengthwise fillet, approximately one-quarter of the whole fish. As with any sashimi, eat bonito sashimi the same day.

SERVES 6–8   200 Cal. per serving

1½–2 lb (685–900 g) very fresh bonito or tuna fillet with skin, if possible
1 clove garlic
½ cup finely grated daikon radish or white radish
1 Tbsp fresh grated ginger
5 green onions, chopped
juice from 1 orange or lemon
hot yellow Japanese mustard (*karashi*) or any hot yellow mustard that is not sweet or vinegary
4 10- to 15-inch (25- to 40-cm) sharp metal skewers
salt

DIPPING SAUCE
6 Tbsps soy sauce
1 Tbsp rice vinegar
1 Tbsp orange juice or ½ Tbsp lemon juice

GARNISHES
1 leek, cut into 2-inch (5-cm) long julienne strips
1 cucumber, sliced into thin julienne strips
1 orange or lemon, thinly sliced

•1. Cut garlic in half. Rub surface of fish with cut side of garlic. Lightly sprinkle fish with salt.

•2. Skewer fillet (see following page) with 4 round metal skewers so that blunt ends of skewers can be held in one hand and skewers fan out into fish. Pass fillet lightly over high open flame one side at a time until red flesh on surface turns white and skin is singed. Maneuver fillet and concentrate heat on portions of flesh and skin that have not turned white or have not been singed until all flesh and skin have been uniformly heated. (This searing protects the flavor.)

•3. Plunge immediately in cold water for 30 to 60 seconds. Remove skewers in a slow twisting motion to prevent fillet from breaking. Remove fish from water and pat dry.

•4. Mix grated daikon, grated ginger, and chopped green onion with pinch salt. Set half of mixture aside for later use. Pat remaining mixture onto flesh side of fish using broad side of a knife. Sprinkle juice from one orange or lemon over fillet and wrap securely in plastic wrap. Refrigerate for 30 minutes to allow fish to cool and absorb flavors.

•5. While fish is cooling, combine DIPPING SAUCE ingredients. Prepare GARNISHES.

•6. Wipe away daikon mixture with your hand and discard. Using a very sharp knife, cut bonito into ½-inch (1½-cm) thick diagonal slices by pulling knife toward you in one long, continuous motion while applying a slight downward pressure (see page 50).

•7. Sprinkle reserved daikon mixture over fish. Arrange sashimi on decorative beds of leek and cucumber. Garnish with orange or lemon slices. Serve with small saucers of dipping sauce and add yellow mustard to taste.

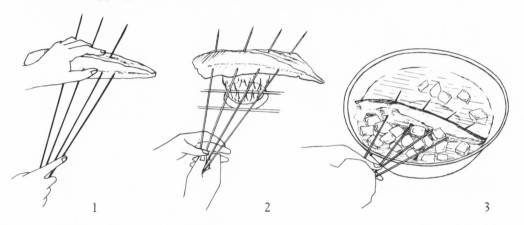

Yellowtail Teriyaki
(Buri teriyaki)

Any fatty fish works well for this recipe. Fish can be grilled, if desired. The fish should be drained well before serving. Yellowtail is at its best in March, and tuna in August. Garnish with turnip chrysanthemums (see page 72) for an added flair. For another teriyaki recipe, see Chicken Teriyaki (page 58).

SERVES 4	299 Cal. per serving

4 yellowtail, salmon, or tuna
   steaks, about 4 oz (115 g) each
3 Tbsps vegetable oil
1½ oz (45 g) thinly sliced sweet
   vinegared ginger, about ⅓ cup
   (optional; see page 27)

MARINADE
4 Tbsps soy sauce
4 Tbsps *mirin*
2 Tbsps saké
1 Tbsp sugar

•1. Combine MARINADE ingredients. Stir until sugar dissolves. Pour marinade over fish, refrigerate, and marinate for 30 to 60 minutes. Turn fish once.

•2. Drain fish and reserve marinade. Heat oil in skillet over medium heat. Add fish and cook until delicately browned (about 2 minutes). Turn once, cover, and reduce heat to low and cook until done (about 4–5 minutes). Remove fish.

•3. In a clean pan, bring marinade to a boil over a high heat. Add fish and coat well, then remove from pan.

•4. Side cooked first is served face up. Garnish with sweet vinegared ginger, and spoon 1 tsp marinade over each fish.

Miso-stuffed Trout

(Nijimasu miso yaki)

Individually wrapped and dressed whole trout are filled with a delicate miso stuffing, then baked until just tender. The trout is served with foil spread slightly to reveal the succulent fish. For an extra touch, garnish with turnip chrysanthemums (page 72).

SERVES 4	323 Cal. per serving

4 rainbow trout, about 5 oz (140 g)
  each
1 Tbsp salt
4 pieces foil, 6 × 8 inches (15 × 20 cm)
oil

MISO STUFFING
4 Tbsps red miso
2 Tbsps sugar
1 Tbsp *mirin*
1 Tbsp secondary bonito stock
1 tsp fresh ginger juice (see page 27)

•1. Scale, clean, and wash trout, leaving head and tail intact. To bone, open fish and insert knife above the backbone at the point closest to the head and run knife lengthwise along bone to release flesh. Repeat to release flesh on other side of bone. Head and tail should still be intact. To remove backbone, sever at points closest to head and tail with knife or scissors, take out backbone, and discard. Check fish for any feather bones and remove with tweezers. Cut off fins along belly. You should have a whole fish with head and tail intact and ready for stuffing. Wash well. Mix salt with 3 cups water in a shallow pan. Soak fish for 5 minutes.

•2. Combine MISO STUFFING ingredients. Cook over medium heat for 4 to 5 minutes, stirring constantly, until slightly thicker than mayonnaise.

•3. Oil each piece of foil and place fish in center. Open fish and spread about 1½ Tbsps miso stuffing in cavity. To prevent stuffing from being squeezed out, fold up foil on belly side first, back side second, then twist ends to secure. Preheat oven to 400°F (205°C) and bake for 12 to 15 minutes. (For larger fish, add 5 minutes cooking time.)

•4. When serving, spread open foil at center so trout can be seen.

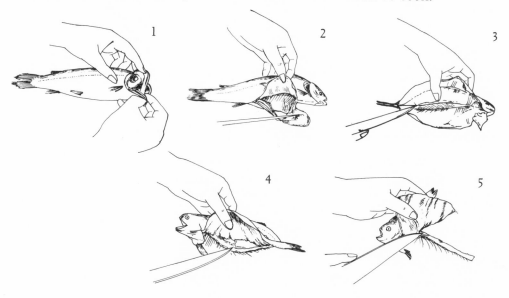

"Riverbank" Oyster Pot

(Kaki dote-nabe)

Try this hearty and nutritious fare on a cold winter evening. Oysters, vegetables, and noodles satisfy the largest of appetites, while the tasty broth warms the whole body. The miso paste is spread around the inside upper edge of the cooking vessel (smaller amounts are mounded in the center) and slowly dissolves into the hot broth, resembling a riverbank sliding into a river. Cook at the table in a deep electric skillet, large fondue pot, or a deep, flameproof (not ovenproof) ceramic casserole (with a tabletop unit). Use a vessel with sloping (rather than vertical) sides, if possible. Oysters shrink if left in too long, so add them last and do not overcook. Fresh clams are also delicious. Goes well with hot steaming rice and Japanese pickles.

SERVES 4	440 Cal. per serving

30 raw oysters, about 14 oz (400 g)
4-inch (10-cm) piece kelp (*konbu*)
3 oz (85 g) cellophane noodles (*harusame*)
3 leeks
1 bunch spinach
1 cake regular tofu, about 10 oz (285 g)
4 leaves Chinese cabbage

MISO PASTE
1 ½ cups red miso, 10 oz (285 g) dry weight
¼ cup sugar
3 Tbsps *mirin*
5 Tbsps saké
1 ½ inches (4 cm) fresh ginger, finely grated (optional)

To prepare

•1. Lightly wipe both sides of kelp with a damp cloth and make ½-inch (1 ½-cm) cuts with scissors at 1-inch (2 ½-cm) intervals (see page 35). Place in a pan containing 5 cups cold water and set aside for 1 hour (for stronger stock, 3 hours). Bring stock to a boil, discard kelp, and remove from heat. Skim off foam.

•2. Combine MISO PASTE ingredients in a saucepan. Stirring constantly, cook over medium heat until mixture thickens and is slightly reduced.

•3. Soak noodles in warm water until soft (10–20 minutes).

•4. Rinse oysters 3 times in cold water to remove as much dirt and residue as possible. Water should no longer be cloudy at the end of 3rd rinsing.
1st rinse: 3 cups water, 1 tsp salt. Stir vigorously. Drain.
2nd rinse: 3 cups water, ½ tsp salt. Stir vigorously. Drain.
3rd rinse: 3 cups water, no salt. Stir vigorously. Drain *well*.

•5. Cut leeks diagonally into ½-inch (1 ½-cm) thick slices. Rinse spinach well in cold water. Drain, then trim off root end. Cut into 2-inch (5-cm) lengths. Cut tofu in half lengthwise, then cut crosswise at ½-inch (1 ½-cm) intervals. Cut cabbage leaves in half lengthwise, then cut crosswise into ½-inch (1 ½-cm) wide strips. Artfully arrange cut ingredients on a large serving platter.

To assemble and eat

•1. For small amounts, mound miso paste in center of electric skillet. For large amounts, spread on inside upper edge of cooking vessel for "riverbank" effect (see color plate, page 9). Add kelp stock, bring to a boil, and reduce to medium heat.

•2. Add some of each ingredient and cook. When vegetables are done, add *some* oysters. Oysters will shrink and become tough if left in stock too long, so add just before eating. Each person removes his or her portion of vegetables and oysters. Replenish pot as portions are removed. Add more stock if the broth begins to taste salty. At the end of the meal dilute broth to taste with hot water (it should be delicate but not too weak) and ladle broth into soup bowls.

Cod in a Pot
(Tara chiri-nabe)

A distinctly different one-pot dish, Cod in a Pot offers toothsome chunks of fish and tofu, and a broth dominated by the natural flavor of cod and supplemented by those of vegetables. Cook at the table and let everyone dig in. Add cooked udon noodles or rice to remaining broth or serve as a soup. Season with salt to taste.

SERVES 4

280 Cal. per serving

4 fresh or quick-frozen cod fillets, about 4 oz (115 g) each
6-inch (15-cm) piece kelp (*konbu*)
2 Tbsps saké
3 leeks
1 bunch spinach
2 cakes regular tofu, about 10 oz (285 g) each

¾ cup finely grated daikon radish or white radish or turnip (step 4)
1 small dried red pepper or ¼ tsp cayenne pepper
4 green onions, finely chopped

LEMON-SOY DIP
½ cup soy sauce
¼ cup lemon juice

•1. Prepare kelp stock 1 to 3 hours in advance, using 2 quarts (2 liters) water (see previous recipe).

•2. Cut cod fillets diagonally into slices 1 inch (2½ cm) wide. Soak in cold water while preparing vegetables. Drain and sprinkle cod with saké before arranging on a separate serving platter.

•3. Prepare leeks, spinach, and tofu (see preceding recipe). Artfully arrange on serving platter.

•4. Peel daikon radish, stuff with red pepper, and grate (see *Shabu-shabu*, page 65, step 6). Place grated daikon in bowl and let each diner mix into lemon-soy dip as desired.

•5. Mix LEMON-SOY DIP ingredients. Divide sauce among 4 small dipping bowls.

•6. Fill cooking vessel two-thirds full of kelp stock (about 4 cups). Bring quickly to a boil, then reduce to simmer. Add enough cod pieces at one time to allow 1 small serving per person. Total cooking time for fish is 5 to 6 minutes. Vegetables are added when fish is nearly done. Each diner transfers his or her own portion to a small bowl containing lemon-soy sauce, adding grated daikon and chopped onion to taste. Replenish fish, vegetables, and kelp stock as needed.

CHICKEN

Chicken Teriyaki
(Tori no teriyaki)

Succulent chicken is marinated and then pan-fried in marinade, sugar, and mirin *to form the delectable teriyaki flavoring known the world over. Simple and authentic. For another teriyaki recipe, see Yellowtail Teriyaki (page 54).*

SERVES 4	410 Cal. per serving

1½ lb (685 g) boned chicken
   thighs or breasts
3 Tbsps oil
1 Tbsp sugar
1 Tbsp *mirin*

MARINADE
3 Tbsps soy sauce
1 Tbsp saké
1 Tbsp *mirin*
1 tsp fresh ginger juice (see page 27)

TURNIP CHRYSANTHEMUM
   (optional)
4 small turnips
4 Tbsps rice vinegar
3 Tbsps sugar
1 small dried red pepper

•1. Prepare optional TURNIP CHRYSANTHEMUM at least 2 or 3 hours in advance (see page 72).

•2. Score chicken in several places so it will lay flat. Pierce both sides of chicken with a fork for better flavor absorption. Mix MARINADE ingredients, add chicken, and set aside for 30 minutes, turning occasionally.

•3. Drain chicken, reserving marinade. Heat oil in skillet until hot. Add chicken, skin side down, and cook over medium heat until skin is crisp and brown. Turn, cover, and reduce to low heat for about 10 minutes. Test chicken by piercing with a fork. When meat is tender and juices are clear, remove meat from pan.

•4. To a clean skillet add sugar, *mirin*, and reserved marinade. Bring quickly to a boil. Add chicken to skillet, flesh side down, for 1 minute and then turn. Wait 30 seconds and turn again. Remove from pan.

•5. Cut into ¾-inch (2-cm) wide slices and arrange on a serving platter. Pour remaining juices over chicken, garnish with turnip chrysanthemums, and serve.

Deep-fried Chicken Nuggets, Japanese Style
(Toriniku tatsuta-age)

These tender nuggets derive their flavor from a ginger-soy sauce marinade, and their crunchy coating from cornstarch and a second deep-frying. Chicken nuggets are delicious as a side dish or hors d'oeuvre, and are great for picnics. The marinade scorches easily, so keep an eye on the chicken while it is cooking.

SERVES 4   307 Cal. per serving

¾ lb (340 g) chicken breast with
  or without skin
2 Tbsps egg white
2 Tbsps cornstarch
3 cups vegetable oil for
  deep-frying
1 large bell pepper

MARINADE
1 ½ Tbsps soy sauce
1 Tbsp saké or *mirin*
1 tsp ginger juice (see page 27)
1 tsp oil

•1. Cut chicken into bite-sized pieces. Combine MARINADE ingredients and then add chicken. Mix well by hand and let stand for 30 minutes.

•2. Add egg white and mix well by hand. Add cornstarch and mix again.

•3. Heat oil in a wok or heavy skillet to medium deep-frying temperature (about 340°F/170°C). Deep-fry a few pieces of chicken at a time. Do not allow chicken to clump together. Turn occasionally. When nuggets rise to the surface, they are done (4–5 minutes). Remove and drain on absorbent paper. Cool.

•4. After nuggets have cooled, reheat oil and refry for 2 to 3 minutes. Remove and drain again on absorbent paper.

•5. Cut bell pepper into 8 pieces. Deep-fry for 1 or 2 minutes until surface of pepper begins to shrivel.

•6. Arrange chicken and bell peppers on platter and serve.

Cold Steamed Chicken with Miso Sauce
(Hiyashi-dori)

Whole chicken breasts are rubbed with fresh lemon, sprinkled with saké, and then steamed with ginger and leek. Try it on a hot summer afternoon. This do-ahead dish is perfect for picnics or an early dinner.

SERVES 4   398 Cal. per serving

2 whole boned chicken breasts with
  skin
2 slices lemon or 1 tsp lemon juice
2 leeks

1 ½ inches (4 cm) fresh ginger
1 Tbsp saké
salt

MISO SAUCE
4 Tbsps miso
1–1½ Tbsps sugar
3 Tbsps *mirin*
2–3 Tbsps rice vinegar
½–1 tsp hot yellow Japanese
  mustard (*karashi*) or any hot
  mustard that is not sweet or
  vinegary

GARNISHES
1 leek
1-inch (2½-cm) length daikon
  radish or 2 oz (60 g) white
  radish or turnip
½ cucumber

•1. Lay chicken skin side up and pierce with fork to allow flavor absorption. Rub both sides with lemon slice (or lemon juice). Sprinkle with salt and saké.

•2. Cut 2 leeks into 1-inch (2½-cm) lengths and then in half lengthwise. Thinly slice ginger. Distribute ginger and leeks under and over chicken in a small baking pan.

•3. Cook, using either of the following methods.

Stove-top method: Steam, using a conventional steamer, a Chinese-style bamboo steamer (see page 73), or a makeshift steamer (page 73). Bring water to a boil and place pan of chicken in steamer. Cover and steam for about 20 minutes over high heat. If steaming in a metal vessel, drape a towel over pot before covering. *Chicken should be tender, and when pierced, the liquid clear.*

Oven method: Preheat oven to 400°F (205°C). Fill a large baking pan with boiling water and place in oven. Cover pan containing chicken with foil, pierce foil in several places, and set covered pan in larger pan of boiling water. Cook for about 20 minutes.

•4. While chicken is cooking, prepare sauce and garnishes.

MISO SAUCE: Combine miso, sugar, and *mirin* in a saucepan. Stir continually over low heat for 5 minutes. Cool. When *cool*, mix in rice vinegar and mustard.

GARNISHES: Cut leek into 2-inch (5-cm) lengths and then in half lengthwise. Slice into fine strips. Peel daikon. Peel and seed cucumber. Shred daikon and cucumber (or slice into fine strips). Soak all garnishes separately in cold water until ready to use.

•5. After cooking chicken, discard leek and ginger, leaving chicken in pan with juices. Wrap pan in foil and refrigerate. Turn chicken occasionally and spoon liquid over top. (Chicken may be placed in freezer to speed up cooling process.) When liquid has congealed, remove meat and cut into ½-inch (1½-cm) thick slices.

•6. Drain garnishes, squeezing out excess moisture by hand. Keeping garnishes separate, make several mounds of each on a large serving platter. Lay chicken slices on a bed of garnish. Spoon any remaining gelatin over chicken, then sauce.

Simmered Chicken and Vegetables
(Iridori)

An economical simmered dish that is simple and satisfying with its variety of tender-crisp vegetables that are first stir-fried and then simmered. Parboiling vegetables separately results in superior flavor. Canned lotus root and bamboo shoots do not require parboiling.

SERVES 4	245 Cal. per serving

4 oz (115 g) boned chicken thighs
   with skin
2 dried *shiitake* mushrooms
4 oz (115 g) burdock, about 10
   inches (25 cm) (if available)
1 medium carrot
10 snow peas
4 oz (115 g) canned bamboo shoots
3 oz (85 g) canned lotus root,
   about 3 inches (8 cm) (optional)
1 tsp chopped fresh ginger
2 Tbsps oil

SIMMERING LIQUID
3 Tbsps soy sauce
3 Tbsps *mirin*
3 Tbsps saké

•1. *Mushrooms*: Soak mushrooms in warm water until soft (about 1 hour), keeping them submerged by covering with drop-lid (see page 91), flat pan lid, or saucer. Discard stems and quarter caps.

Burdock: Scrub well with a stiff brush under running water but do not scrape or peel. Cut into bite-sized wedges by making a crosswise diagonal cut near the tip, rotating a quarter turn, and cutting again. Parboil.

Carrot: Peel and cut into bite-sized wedges in same manner as burdock. Parboil.

Snow peas: Remove stem and strings and blanch in boiling water (about 1 minute).

Bamboo shoots: Wash well and remove any white residue. Cut crosswise at a slight diagonal into bite-sized pieces.

Lotus root: Cut into rounds and quarter.

Chicken: Cut into bite-sized pieces.

•2. Heat oil. Stir-fry firmer vegetables first. Add burdock and lotus, stir a few seconds, add bamboo shoots, stir 30 seconds, and then add carrot and mushroom. (Reserve snow peas for garnish.) Continue to stir-fry over medium-high heat for 2 to 3 minutes until *almost* tender-crisp. Remove vegetables, but retain pan juices in skillet.

•3. Add SIMMERING LIQUID to pan juices and bring to a boil over medium heat. Mix in ginger and chicken, coating chicken thoroughly. When chicken darkens (about 1 minute), remove from pan and again retain pan juices.

•4. Return vegetables to skillet and simmer over low heat until liquid is nearly absorbed. Add chicken and continue to simmer until all liquid is absorbed. Garnish with snow peas and serve.

Chicken Roll
(Maki-dori)

This colorful dish appears difficult to assemble but is actually quite easy. Chicken breasts are stuffed with asparagus, shrimp, and scrambled egg, then rolled, baked, and glazed. Colorful, exotic, and simple.

SERVES 4   428 Cal. per serving

2 whole boned chicken breasts with
   or without skin
4 fresh green asparagus stalks
7 oz (200 g) shrimp
1 Tbsp sugar
2 eggs
vegetable oil
2 tsps cornstarch
1½ oz (45 g) thinly sliced sweet
   vinegared ginger, about ⅓ cup
   (optional; see page 27)
salt
toothpicks

GLAZE
1 Tbsp soy sauce
1 Tbsp *mirin*

To prepare and assemble

•1. Cut off tough portions of asparagus stalks and discard. Parboil asparagus in lightly salted water.

•2. Score chicken lengthwise down the middle, penetrating about halfway through breast. Turn knife to the left and score at least once to flatten and increase surface area of breast. Repeat on the right side.

•3. Remove shell and tail of shrimp. Devein (see page 38) and chop coarsely. Sprinkle with ¼ tsp salt and 1 tsp sugar.

•4. Scramble eggs with 2 tsps sugar and pinch salt, stirring constantly with a fork or wire whisk, until eggs are nearly firm and dry.

•5. Lay chicken breasts skin side down. Lightly sprinkle with cornstarch and salt. Place 2 asparagus spears *crosswise* down center of each chicken breast. Spoon shrimp over asparagus and place egg alongside shrimp. Roll and secure with toothpicks.

To cook and serve

•1. Line a roasting pan with foil and oil lightly. Place rolls on pan, seam side down. Bake in preheated oven at 400°F (205°C) for 12 to 15 minutes.

•2. While chicken is baking, mix GLAZE ingredients and bring to a boil over medium heat. When chicken has turned a light golden brown (after 12–15 minutes), brush on glaze. Return chicken to oven until it turns a dark golden brown.

Brush on glaze again, return to oven for a couple of minutes, remove, and brush on glaze one final time.

•**3.** Slice crosswise into ½-inch (1½-cm) thick rounds and, keeping slices together, fan out slightly, one slice overlapping the one behind it. Slices can also be stacked pyramid-style. Garnish with sweet vinegared ginger. Serve hot or at room temperature.

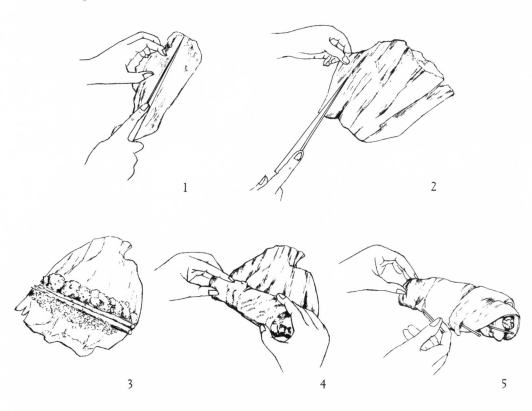

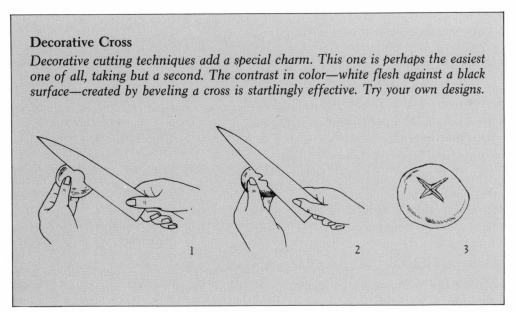

Decorative Cross

Decorative cutting techniques add a special charm. This one is perhaps the easiest one of all, taking but a second. The contrast in color—white flesh against a black surface—created by beveling a cross is startlingly effective. Try your own designs.

BEEF AND PORK

Shabu-shabu

This dish is not soon forgotten. Shabu-shabu *derives its name from the sound of the meat as it is swished in simmering broth. The secret to success lies in the thinness and quality of the meat, and the few seconds it takes to cook. The dipping sauces provide stimulating contrasts in taste, while the assortment of fresh vegetables and the noodle finale make this a hearty, well-balanced meal that requires only the accompaniment of dessert and hot tea for perfection.*

SERVES 4   1047 Cal. per serving

1 ¼ lb (570 g) well-marbled
  sirloin, sliced paper thin
2 quarts (2 liters) bonito stock
  (primary or secondary)
4 leaves Chinese cabbage
12–16 fresh young spinach leaves
  with stems
3 leeks
1 cake regular tofu, about 10 oz
  (285 g)
8 fresh *shiitake* mushrooms or
  12–16 white mushrooms
4 servings *udon* noodles (optional)
1 small dried red pepper or ¼ tsp
  cayenne pepper
¾ cup finely grated daikon radish
  or white radish or turnip (see
  step 6)
4–5 green onions, finely chopped

LEMON-SOY DIP
2-inch (5-cm) piece kelp (*konbu*)
5 Tbsps soy sauce
2 Tbsps rice vinegar
1 Tbsp fresh lemon juice

SESAME SAUCE
½ cup secondary bonito stock
6 Tbsps white sesame seeds
2 Tbsps white miso
2 Tbsps *mirin*
2 tsps soy sauce
2 tsps rice vinegar
1 clove garlic
pinch red pepper
2 tsps vegetable oil

To prepare

•1. Prepare a total of 8½ cups bonito stock.

•2. Blanch 4 whole cabbage leaves in boiling water until soft, then cool in cold water. Drain. Pare down thick veins (see page 93) so cabbage can be rolled. Blanch spinach in same manner as cabbage. Squeeze out excess moisture. Place 3 or 4 spinach leaves at core end of cabbage leaf and roll up. Trim excess stem. Cut rolls into 1½-inch (4-cm) sections and stand on end on serving platter.

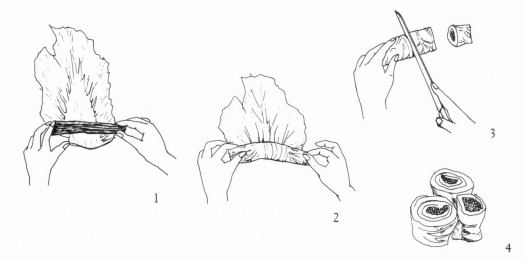

•**3.** Cut leeks diagonally into 1-inch (2½-cm) pieces. Cut tofu into bite-sized cubes. Wash and trim mushrooms. (If using fresh *shiitake* mushrooms, discard stems and wash caps.) Artfully arrange on serving platter. Neatly lay out strips of beef on a separate platter.

•**4.** If desired, cook *udon* noodles (see page 109).

•**5.** LEMON-SOY DIP: Lightly wipe both sides of kelp with a damp cloth and make ½-inch (1½-cm) cuts with scissors at 1-inch (2½-cm) intervals (see page 35). In a saucepan combine kelp with remaining sauce ingredients. Set aside for 10 minutes. Do not heat. Remove kelp.

•**6.** Soften dried red pepper in water, then clip off large end and squeeze out seeds. Peel daikon. With a sturdy chopstick (or similar utensil) poke a hole lengthwise through the center of daikon and then stuff in whole pepper. (This will enable you to grate the pepper when you grate the daikon.) Finely grate daikon and red pepper. The result will be reddish in color. (If using cayenne pepper, simply grate daikon and mix in pepper.) Place grated daikon mixture in bowl and let each diner mix into lemon-soy dip as desired.

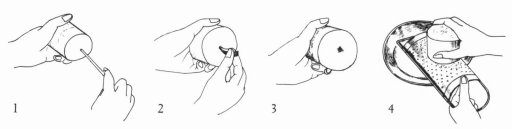

•**7.** SESAME SAUCE: Toast and grind sesame seeds (see page 30). Dice and mash garlic. To sesame seed, add miso, *mirin*, soy sauce, rice vinegar, garlic, and pepper. Mix well. Add oil. Mix. Blend in bonito stock. (For a slight variation of SESAME SAUCE, see Mixed Grill, page 67.)

To cook

In Japan *Shabu-shabu* is cooked at the table in an earthenware casserole (*donabe*) or a Mongolian hot-pot (*hoko-nabe*), but it is possible to obtain good results using a deep electric skillet. If a tabletop heating unit is available, use a heavy 3-quart (3-liter) flameproof (not ovenproof) casserole.

Provide every diner with a bowl of each dipping sauce. Add daikon-and-red pepper mixture (to lemon-soy dip only) and finely chopped green onions as desired.

Pour bonito stock into cooking vessel until two-thirds full and heat until just boiling. Each diner uses his or her own chopsticks to pick up a thin slice of beef and swish it in the bonito stock, cooking it to taste. The meat takes only a few seconds to cook, but the vegetables take more time, so drop the vegetables in and let them cook a while. Skim off foam occasionally.

After all the meat and vegetables have been eaten, reheat noodles (see page 109), divide remaining broth among 4 large soup bowls, add noodles, top with finely chopped green onions, and serve. Season to taste with salt and pepper. The broth can also be served alone, lightly seasoned to taste.

Mixed Grill
(Teppan-yaki)

Two kinds of dipping sauce, an assortment of fresh vegetables and seafood, and thinly sliced (or cubed) beef compose this family-style dish cooked at the table on an electric griddle or in a skillet on a tabletop unit. Ingredients are easily added or substituted (see variations) and amounts adjusted, so tailor this meal to your own whims, selecting the freshest seasonal vegetables and seafood. For party suggestions, see Mixed Grill Party (page 149).

SERVES 4	700 Cal. per serving

1–1½ lb (450–685 g) tenderloin or
   sirloin, thinly sliced or cubed
1 eggplant, about 10 oz (285 g)
1 potato
½ medium sweet potato
4 cabbage leaves
8 fresh *shiitake* mushrooms or
   12–16 white mushrooms
2 onions
1 bell pepper
7 oz (200 g) fresh bean sprouts
4 prawns or 4 large scallops
½ cup finely grated daikon or
   white radish or turnip (see step 3)
1 small dried red pepper or ¼ tsp
   cayenne pepper
vegetable oil for grilling

SESAME SAUCE
3 Tbsps white sesame seeds
6 Tbsps soy sauce
2 Tbsps *mirin*
2 Tbsps fresh lemon juice
2 Tbsps secondary bonito stock

LEMON-SOY DIP
6 Tbsps soy sauce
4 Tbsps fresh lemon juice

To prepare

•1. Prepare ingredients as instructed below and decoratively arrange on one or more large serving platters.

Eggplant: Slice into ¼-inch (¾-cm) rounds. If eggplant is especially large, cut in half or quarters lengthwise, then slice. Soak in cold water for 15 to 20 minutes. Pat dry with cloth.

Potato: Peel and slice into ¼-inch (¾-cm) rounds. Soak for 5 minutes to remove starch and then pat dry.

Sweet potato: Wash and slice into ¼-inch (¾-cm) rounds. Wash again and pat dry.

Cabbage: Pare down vein on each leaf (see page 93). Roll up leaves and slice into ½-inch (1½-cm) wide strips.

Mushrooms: Wash well. Trim inedible portion of stems, then cut mushrooms in half lengthwise (or discard stems and grill whole caps). If using fresh *shiitake* mushrooms, discard stems and grill whole caps (or cup in half, if desired).

Onions: Slice crosswise into ¼-inch (¾-cm) rounds.

Bell pepper: Seed and quarter.

Bean sprouts: Wash and drain well.

Prawns: Shell and devein (see page 38). For better flavor, leave shell intact and devein by inserting toothpick at second joint.

Beef: Neatly lay out strips on a separate serving platter or cut in a bite-sized cubes.

•2. SESAME SAUCE: Toast and grind sesame seeds (see page 30). Mix in remaining ingredients. Divide among 4 small dipping bowls. (For a variation of sesame sauce, see *Shabu-shabu*, page 65.)

•3. Peel daikon, stuff with red pepper, and finely grate (see page 65, step 6).

•4. Combine LEMON-SOY DIP ingredients, then strain through cheesecloth to remove pulp. Divide lemon-soy dip among 4 small dipping bowls. Place grated daikon mixture in a bowl and let each diner mix in a lemon-soy dip as desired.

To cook

Provide every diner with a bowl of each dipping sauce. Set griddle or skillet temperature to 400°F (205°C). Use an oil-saturated cloth to lightly coat cooking surface. Grill desired items, oiling surface as often as necessary so food does not stick. There is no definite cooking order or time, but no item should take more than 7 or 8 minutes. Eat the items hot off the grill.

VARIATIONS: Boned chicken, sliced pork, or thin lamb chops can be added or substituted for beef. Oysters, clams in their shells, carrots, and corn on the cob all make good additions.

Sukiyaki

Ironically, this dish—arguably the most popular of Japanese dishes outside Japan—evolved only after foreign diplomats introduced beef to a skeptical fish-eating populace. Cook it at the table and allow each diner to choose whatever he or she likes from the succulent mouthfuls simmering in the flavorful broth. Hot rice makes a good accompaniment.

14 oz to 1 ¼ lb (400–570 g) well-
    marbled, thinly sliced sirloin
2–2 ½ oz (60–70 g) beef suet
4 dried *shiitake* mushrooms
3 leeks
7 oz (200 g) fresh spinach
1 cake regular tofu, about 10 oz
    (285 g)
10 oz (285 g) Chinese cabbage
5 oz (140 g) *shirataki* filaments or
    3 oz (85 g) cellophane noodles
    (*harusame*)
4 eggs

COOKING BROTH
½ cup kelp (*konbu*) stock made
    with 6-inch (15-cm) piece kelp
    (see steps 2 and 3)
½ cup soy sauce
½ cup *mirin*
3 Tbsps sugar

To prepare

•1. Soak mushrooms in warm water until soft (about 1 hour), keeping them submerged by covering with drop-lid (see page 91), flat pan lid, or saucer. Drain. Discard stem and notch a decorative cross design on caps.

•2. Lightly wipe both sides of kelp with a damp cloth and make ½-inch (1 ½-cm) cuts with scissors at 1-inch (2 ½-cm) intervals (see page 35). Soak in 1 ½ cups water for 30 minutes to make kelp stock.

•3. Remove ½ cup of kelp stock and combine with remaining COOKING BROTH ingredients. Bring to a boil. Transfer to a small pitcher that can be easily used at the table. Reserve remaining kelp stock to thin out cooking broth.

•4. Cut leeks diagonally into 1-inch (2 ½-cm) lengths. Cut spinach into 2-inch (5-cm) lengths. Cut tofu into bite-sized cubes. Cut Chinese cabbage crosswise into 1 ½-inch (4-cm) wide strips. Roughly chop *shirataki* filaments and parboil in boiling water for 30 seconds or pour boiling water over filaments. (If using cellophane noodles, soak in warm water until soft—10 to 20 minutes.) Artfully arrange on one or more serving platters. Neatly lay out strips of beef on a separate dish.

To cook

Heat the electric skillet to 400°F (205°C). Melt suet in skillet, coating well. Fill one-quarter of the skillet with sliced beef, spreading out the slices so meat will cook through. This is a "cook as you go" dish, so add the other ingredients only in amounts that can be eaten in a few minutes, filling the gaps as food is eaten. Pour in enough broth to cover the bottom of the skillet, but not so much as to completely submerge beef and vegetables. Add kelp stock and any remaining cooking broth as liquid in the skillet evaporates, adjusting flavor to taste.

Provide a small bowl and a raw egg for each diner. Beat egg lightly with fork or chopsticks. This is the dipping sauce. The hot food "lightly cooks" the egg.

NOTE: A delicious and easy-to-make dish called Beef Bowl (*Gyudon*) can be made with Sukiyaki leftovers. Stir-fry vegetables and then beef. Serve in a large bowl over hot cooked rice.

Beef Tartare, Japanese Style

(Gyuniku no tataki)

The pleasure of enjoying beef at the height of its flavor is the beauty of this dish. The painlessly simple preparation successfully seals in meat juices with surprising results, and the dipping sauce accentuates the fresh flavor. Goes well with Tofu Steak (page 82).

SERVES 4	315 Cal. per serving

14 oz (400 g) high-quality sirloin
   tips or lean round steak, about
   1 ½ inches (4 cm) thick
salt and pepper
2 Tbsps vegetable oil
1 Tbsp saké or brandy
1 cup finely grated daikon radish
   or white radish or turnip

DIPPING SAUCE
1 clove garlic
⅓ onion, finely grated
5 Tbsps soy sauce
2 Tbsps wine vinegar
1 Tbsp vegetable oil
1 Tbsp *mirin*

GARNISHES (optional)
½ cucumber
½ carrot
1 rib celery
4–6 lettuce leaves

To prepare and cook

•1. Sprinkle beef with salt and pepper. In a skillet heat oil over high heat. Sear beef for 30 seconds on each side until just browned.

•2. Pour saké or brandy over all and ignite. When flame dies away, remove meat from heat. The outside will be nicely browned and the inside raw. Cool.

•3. Seal in plastic wrap and refrigerate until just chilled or for as long as 2 days, according to taste.

•4. While meat is cooling, prepare vegetables. Peel and seed cucumber. Peel carrot. Shred. (These will become a decorative bed for the meat.) Soak each vegetable separately in cold water until ready to use.

•5. Dice and mash garlic, and combine with remaining DIPPING SAUCE ingredients.

To serve

Cut beef against the grain into ¼-inch (¾-cm) thick slices. Line serving dish with lettuce. Drain shredded vegetables well and squeeze out excess water by hand. Mound decoratively on serving dish. Place sliced beef on beds of vegetables (or place meat in center of serving dish and garnish edges with shredded vegetables). Sprinkle grated daikon over meat with a spoon. Provide a small bowl of dipping sauce for each diner.

Ginger Pork Sauté
(Butaniku shoga-yaki)

Sautéed pork is accented with the zesty juice of fresh ginger, elegantly garnished with edible turnip chrysanthemums, and crowned with rings of pineapple. Omit the optional turnips and this dish is easily prepared on short notice.

SERVES 4   462 Cal. per serving

12–14 oz (340–400 g) pork shoulder, thinly sliced into 4 portions, or 4 thin pork loin cutlets
2 Tbsps soy sauce
1 Tbsp *mirin*
2 tsps fresh ginger juice (see page 27)
1 Tbsp flour
2 ½ Tbsps oil
4 slices canned pineapple (optional)
4 lettuce leaves (optional garnish)

TURNIP CHRYSANTHEMUM (optional)
4 small turnips
4 Tbsps rice vinegar
3 Tbsps sugar
1 small dried red pepper

SEASONING
2 Tbsps soy sauce
2 tsps sugar
2 tsps *mirin*

To prepare

•1. Prepare TURNIP CHRYSANTHEMUM at least 2 or 3 hours in advance (page 72).

•2. Combine soy sauce, *mirin*, and 1 tsp ginger juice. Sprinkle over pork. Let stand for 10 minutes.

•3. Dredge both sides of pork with flour. (A tea strainer works well for this.)

To cook and serve

•1. Heat frying pan until very hot. Add 2 Tbsps oil and reheat. Sauté pork on both sides until lightly browned. Remove pork.

•2. Wash pan and add SEASONING ingredients. Bring to a boil over medium heat and add pork. Sprinkle with 1 tsp ginger juice. When pork is well coated with mixture, it is done.

•3. Wash pan again. Heat ½ Tbsp oil and sauté pineapple rings until lightly browned. Shake pan occasionally to prevent sticking.

•4. Line serving platter with lettuce leaves. Decoratively arrange pork, turnip chrysanthemums, and pineapple rings.

Pork or Beef Marinade
(Niku no miso-zuke)

A wonderful do-ahead dish, Pork or Beef Marinade is ideal for those with a busy schedule. The meat is best after 2 or 3 days but will keep as long as 1 week tightly sealed in plastic wrap and refrigerated. The marinade can be reused twice. Garnish with turnip chrysanthemums (see page 72) for an extra flourish.

8 pork chops, ½ inch (1½ cm)
   thick *or*
8 small steaks, 3–4 oz (85–115 g)
   each *or*
4 pork chops and 4 small steaks
7 oz (200 g) bean sprouts
2 bell peppers
4 Tbsps vegetable oil
½ tsp salt

MARINADE
5 Tbsps red miso
2 Tbsps *mirin*
1 Tbsp sugar
2 Tbsps saké

To prepare

•1. Tenderize meat with a mallet.

•2. Mix MARINADE ingredients by hand in a shallow glass or enamel pan. Do not use a metal pan. Coat meat well with marinade, arrange in a single layer, and cover with plastic wrap. Refrigerate 2 to 3 days.

To cook

•1. Soak bean sprouts in cold water until ready to use. Seed bell peppers and cut into fine strips.

•2. Remove meat from refrigerator. Wipe away most of marinade by hand and grill in a broiler or pan-fry in an oiled skillet. Cook pork 2 or 3 minutes on each side. Grill beef to taste.

•3. Drain bean sprouts well. Heat 2 Tbsps oil and stir-fry bean sprouts and bell peppers together. Sprinkle with ½ tsp salt.

•4. Top meat with vegetables and serve.

Soft Simmered Pork
(Buta kaku-ni)

This method renders pork wonderfully tender, making it possible to break into bite-sized pieces with just chopsticks.

2–2¼ lb (about 1 kg) boneless
   pork plate spare ribs or fat back,
   cut into 8 pieces
4 Tbsps soy sauce
2 Tbsps oil
4 inches (10 cm) fresh ginger
½ cup saké

4 Tbsps sugar
½ tsp salt
hot yellow Japanese mustard
   (*karashi*) or any hot mustard
   that is not sweet or vinegary
   (optional)

To prepare

•1. Sprinkle pork with 1 Tbsp soy sauce. Sauté in hot oil until brown on both sides. Transfer immediately to a pan of boiling water for 30 seconds (or pour boiling water over pork) to remove excess oil. Drain.

•2. Peel ginger. Slice 2½ inches (6½ cm) into several pieces and crush with a tenderizing mallet or the side of a knife. Cut remaining ginger into very fine slivers and reserve until last step.

•3. Place pork, crushed ginger, saké, and 7 cups water in a pressure cooker or heavy saucepan. Simmer 40 minutes in pressure cooker or 3 hours in covered saucepan over low heat.

•4. Let pork cool (or force-cool) until fat congeals on surface. Skim off fat.

Turnip Chrysanthemum

This garnish has all the qualities necessary to make it a popular and useful addition to any Western kitchen. It is ingenious yet simple to make, attractive, edible, and keeps 1 week refrigerated in a bowl of sweet vinegar. Make it in a spare moment and serve it as a garnish, as an hors d'oeuvre, or pull it out in an emergency and set it out as a side dish. Begin preparation at least 2½ hours in advance. See color plate for Ginger Pork Sauté (page 10).

4 small turnips
4 Tbsps rice vinegar
3 Tbsps sugar
1 small dried red pepper

1. Peel turnips and cut off tops about ½ inch (1 cm) below stem. Discard tops and trim bottoms of turnips so each is flat. Place one turnip, top side down, on a cutting board between a pair of wooden chopsticks. (These will prevent cutting completely through turnip.) Score at right angle to chopsticks as fine as possible and as deeply as chopsticks will allow. Turn turnip 90° and score crosswise in the same manner. Turn turnip over and make 8 to 10 slashes with a knife.

2. Soak in salted water (1 tsp salt for every cup water) for 30 minutes to soften. (If you are in a hurry, you can shorten softening time by rubbing each side with salt, setting aside for 10 minutes, then rinsing.)

3. Gently squeeze to remove excess moisture and soak "petal" side down in vinegar and sugar (sweet vinegar) for 2 to 3 hours or refrigerate overnight.

4. To serve, hold petal side down and gently squeeze out vinegar. Place turnip, petal side down, in left hand (if you are right-handed) and, holding left hand stationary, apply slight pressure with right hand and twist. This will spread the petals. Soften red pepper in water, then chop off large end and squeeze out seeds. Slice into thin rounds. Place one round of red pepper in center of each turnip flower.

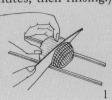 

1   2   3   4

To cook and serve

•1. Transfer pork and as much broth as possible to metal bowl. Add sugar, salt, and 3 Tbsps soy sauce.

•2. Cover bowl with foil and pierce foil. Set bowl in a large pan of boiling water and cook in preheated oven at 390°F (200°C) for 1 to 1½ hours, according to taste. Meat can also be steamed, using a conventional steamer, Chinese-style bamboo steamer (see below), or a makeshift steamer (below). *Check water level periodically and replenish with boiling water if necessary.*

•3. For a thicker broth, simmer broth only over a medium heat until desired thickness is achieved.

•4. Serve whole pieces. Spoon on 1 Tbsp broth and sprinkle on fine slivers of fresh ginger. Serve with a dab of hot yellow mustard, if desired.

CHINESE-STYLE STEAMER: These round bamboo-slatted steamers with wooden sides are efficient and inexpensive. The woven bamboo cover insulates well yet very little moisture accumulates on its underside, unlike conventional metal steamers and the makeshift steamer where a towel must be used to absorb moisture and prevent it from dripping down on to the food being steamed.

Used in tandem with a wok, the steamer is placed in the wok after several inches of water have been brought to a boil. Food placed in a pan, dish, or cup is then added. Cover and steam according to directions. Remove food only after steam has dissipated.

Available in various sizes at Chinese provision stores throughout the United States, medium-sized steamers 10 to 12 inches (25 to 30 cm) in diameter are best for household use. Although one tier and a cover will satisfy all the needs of this book, a second tier is useful for steaming two different things simultaneously, reheating leftovers, and so on.

To break in a bamboo steamer, soak it in water for 2 or 3 hours. After using, wash well with water *only* and allow it to dry completely before storing it, unwrapped, in a dry place. Keep steamer out of direct sunlight.

MAKESHIFT STEAMER: If there is no steamer at hand, improvise one with a large pot and several heat-resistant cups (or empty cans with both ends cut away): Place two or three heat-resistant cups (or cans), open end up, in pot. Fill pot and cups with water but stop at least 1 inch (2½ cm) below lip of cups (to allow for action of boiling water). Bring water to a boil, then carefully place pan with foods to be steamed on cups. Drape a kitchen towel over pot to prevent condensed moisture from dripping onto food. Cover, but allow steam to escape (to minimize condensation and prevent pressure build up). Fold loose corners of towel up over pot lid (to keep ends away from flames). Steam according to directions. When done, turn off heat and allow steam to dissipate before removing food.

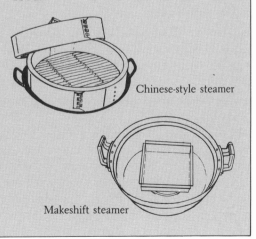

Chinese-style steamer

Makeshift steamer

Thousand-layer Rolled Omelette
(Dashi-make tamago)

In Japan a rectangular omelette pan (makiyaki nabe) is used to facilitate rolling. Any omelette pan or conventional frying pan along with a bamboo rolling mat (or kitchen towel) for shaping the egg can be used to achieve the same result, although an unscarred pan that allows easy maneuvering of the egg is necessary to produce an omelette with a many-layered effect. Serve for breakfast or as an appetizer. Egg should be soft and pliant, not dry and rubbery.

SERVES 4	208 Cal. per serving

6 eggs
6–8 Tbsps primary bonito stock
1 tsp soy sauce
1 tsp *mirin*
1 Tbsp sugar
⅓ tsp salt
2 Tbsps vegetable oil

CONDIMENTS
½ cup finely grated daikon radish
   or white radish or turnip
¼ cup finely grated cucumber
   (optional)
1½ oz (45 g) thinly sliced sweet
   vinegared ginger, about ⅓ cup
   (see page 27)

•1. Beat eggs well, frothing as little as possible. Add bonito stock, soy sauce, *mirin*, sugar, and salt.

•2. Heat a 6- to 8-inch (15- to 20-cm) skillet or egg pan over medium-high heat until medium-hot. Lightly oil pan using a paper towel or cloth swab. Pour enough egg mixture into pan to cover bottom (¼ to ⅓ cup) and tilt pan to coat evenly. Stir lightly, breaking any bubbles, until nearly set (center top will still be runny). Tilt pan towards you and roll up egg with spatula (or roll away from you, if easier).

Re-oil pan surface, slide rolled egg to farthest end, finish re-oiling, and add more egg mixture. Lift rolled egg and tilt pan slightly so that uncooked egg will flow under rolled egg. When new egg is done, start with previously rolled egg and repeat rolling process to make one large roll.

Cook remaining egg in same manner. The number of times this process has to be repeated depends on the size of the pan. Adjust heat when necessary to allow quick, even cooking without browning. Remember, egg should be soft and pliant, not rubbery. Brown last batch slightly.

•3. Wrap egg in cheesecloth and then in bamboo rolling mat (see page 130) or dry kitchen towel folded several times. Press gently into a rectangular shape. (This may take a few minutes.) If serving chilled or at room temperature, let cool before slicing.

•4. Unwrap and trim ends of roll, if necessary. Cut omelette roll crosswise into 1-inch (2 ½ -cm) slices.

•5. Combine grated daikon and cucumber. Drain off water. Mound on plate and place sliced egg alongside. Season grated condiments with soy sauce to taste. Garnish with a few pieces of sweet vinegared ginger. Serve hot, chilled, or at room temperature.

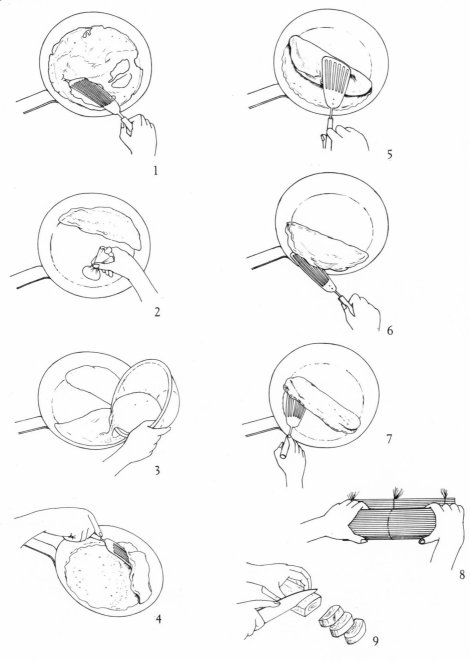

Egg "Tofu" Custard
(Tamago-dofu)

Light and savory, this egg custard will delight those who favor a delicate taste. For an added touch, garnish with crisp cucumber rounds or any colorful fresh fruit, such as strawberries or cherries. Note that the volume of egg (not the number of eggs) is important and must always equal the volume of broth. Serve this popular summer egg custard hot or cold.

SERVES 4   157 Cal. per serving

1½ cups egg, about 6 medium
   eggs

BROTH
1½ cups primary bonito stock
1 tsp *mirin*
½ tsp salt
½ tsp soy sauce

CONDIMENTS
¼ cup chopped green onion
wasabi horseradish

SAUCE
⅔ cup primary bonito stock
1 Tbsp *mirin*
1 Tbsp soy sauce
¼ tsp salt

To prepare

•1. Prepare 2¼ cups bonito stock.

•2. Combine BROTH ingredients, and, stirring occasionally, bring to a boil over medium heat, making sure that salt dissolves. Force-cool by swirling bowl with broth in a larger bowl containing water and ice cubes.

•3. Beat eggs gently until whites and yolks are well mixed. Slowly add *cooled* broth to egg while continuing to mix.

•4. Moisten a 6- × -6-inch (15- × -15-cm) baking pan with water and line with plastic wrap or foil. (If using oven method, do not use plastic wrap.) Wrap should be as wrinkle-free as possible. Pass egg mixture through cheesecloth-lined strainer into baking pan. Skim off any foam. Cook according to one of the following methods.

Stove-top method: Steam, using a conventional steamer, a Chinese-style bamboo steamer (see page 73), or a makeshift steamer (page 73). Bring water to a boil, place uncovered pan containing egg mixture in steamer, and cover. If steaming in a metal vessel, drape a towel over pot before covering. Steam for 2 minutes over high heat, then reduce to low and steam until mixture sets (about 15 minutes). *Insert a toothpick in middle to test custard. When done, toothpick will come out clean. Unlike real tofu, egg "tofu" should be soft and delicate in consistency, not firm and dry.*

Oven method: Preheat oven to 325°F (165°C). Cover pan containing egg mixture with foil and pierce foil every 2 inches (5 cm). Place covered pan in a large pan, fill with *boiling* water to a level half the height of the inner pan, and cook until mixture sets (15–20 minutes).

•5. Combine SAUCE ingredients and bring to a boil over medium heat, making sure salt dissolves. Force-cool by placing saucepan in cold water.

To remove and serve

•1. After cooking, immerse baking pan in cold water. (If using oven method, remove top foil before setting pan in cold water.)

•2. When cool, run a knife around the edge of the pan (still immersed in water) to loosen custard. Gently lift custard out of pan by grabbing the ends of the plastic wrap or foil and remove pan from water. Keeping custard immersed in water and supporting it from underneath with one hand, slowly peel away wrap and cut (or carefully lift out of water with plastic wrap, place on cutting board, and cut), and place directly on serving plates, allowing each piece to drain as you lift it out of the water. (Trim messy edges, if desired.) Custard is fragile and breaks apart easily, so handle carefully.

•3. Serve topped with sauce and green onion or *wasabi* horseradish. Egg custard can be eaten hot or cold. To reheat soak custard in hot water. Do not use boiling water. To serve sauce hot, reheat by bringing to a boil and thickening with cornstarch dissolved in 1 Tbsp water.

Savory Dinner Egg Custard
(Chawan-mushi)

This dinner custard is to sweet dessert custard what a dinner crepe is to its dessert counterpart: a delectable variation appropriate during the main meal. Ingredients are rendered wonderfully tender cooked in the custard. Pick out morsels and savor their brothy succulence. Ham can be substituted for chicken and bamboo shoots for mushrooms.

SERVES 4

119 Cal. per serving

3 eggs
4 dried *shiitake* mushrooms
4 oz (115 g) boned chicken breast
   without skin
1 tsp soy sauce
1 tsp saké
8 small raw shrimp
salt and saké to season shrimp
2 leaves fresh young spinach
   without stem or 4 snow peas

SEASONING
2 cups primary bonito stock
1 tsp soy sauce
1 tsp *mirin*
½ tsp salt

To prepare

•1. Soak mushrooms in warm water until soft (about 1 hour), keeping them submerged by covering with drop-lid (see page 91), flat pan lid, or saucer. Drain. Discard stems and notch a decorative cross on each mushroom cap (see page 63).

•**2.** Combine SEASONING ingredients and bring to a boil over a medium heat. Remove from heat and cool.

•**3.** *Chicken*: Remove any fat from breast and cut into 8 pieces. Mix saké and soy sauce and sprinkle over chicken pieces.

Shrimp: Shell and devein (see page 38), leaving tail intact. Sprinkle with salt and a little saké.

Vegetable: Blanch spinach in boiling water and cut into 2-inch (5-cm) lengths. If using snow peas, string and blanch in boiling water, then cut in half.

•**4.** Beat eggs, frothing as little as possible. Mix in *cooled* seasoning broth and strain through cheesecloth.

To cook and serve

•**1.** Divide mixture evenly among 4 cups (use custard cups or heat-resistant coffee mugs). Add chicken, carefully position shrimp so that tail peeks out of egg mixture, add vegetables, and float a whole mushroom cap (beveled side up).

•**2.** Cook, using one of the following methods.

Stove-top method: Steam, using a conventional steamer, a Chinese-style bamboo steamer (see page 73), or a makeshift steamer (page 73). Bring water to a boil. Place uncovered cups in steamer. If steaming in a metal vessel, drape a towel over pot before covering. Cover and steam 2 minutes over high heat, then reduce to low and steam until set. Total steaming time will be 15 to 20 minutes. *It is done when a toothpick inserted in the middle comes out clean. The surface of the custard should have a smooth (not dry and cracked) look.*

Oven method: Preheat oven to 400°F (205°C). Cover cups with foil and pierce foil. Set cups in a pan and fill with boiling water to a level one-third the height of cups. Place cups in pan and cook for 10 minutes. Reduce heat to 360°F (180°C) and continue to cook until set. Total cooking time will be about 25 to 30 minutes.

•**3.** Remove foil if using oven method. Ideally, for decorative purposes, shrimp and at least one other ingredient should be peeping out (see color plate, page 12). Serve hot or chilled in cup.

TOFU

Homemade Tofu

Ultimate freshness and flavor—that is what making tofu is all about. Unless you are extremely fortunate, the local tofu will not have the smooth, creamy texture and the delicate flavor found in very fresh homemade tofu. Making tofu at home also yields a high-protein byproduct known as okara, or tofu pulp, an almost flavorless food substance that absorbs other flavors extremely well and supplies bulk and roughage. (For a recipe using okara, see Okara and Vegetable Mélange, page 86.)

Proper storage of tofu is essential. Float tofu in a container of water, cover to prevent absorption of food odors, and refrigerate. Homemade tofu should be eaten within 2 or 3 days. (Packaged tofu keeps 3 to 5 days.)

MAKES 1 LARGE DENSE CAKE,
ABOUT 28 OUNCES (800 GRAMS)   373 Cal. per 10 ounces

1½ cups dry soybeans
water reserved from soaking beans
2 level tsps calcium sulfate (this
    coagulant is available at .phar-
    macies and healthfood stores)

SPECIAL EQUIPMENT
thermometer
large cheesecloth or bag-shaped
    cheesecloth
colander (not wire mesh), tofu box
    (shown), or 1-quart (1-liter)
    plastic container with drainage
    holes in sides and bottom

•1. Wash and sort soybeans. Soak in 4½ cups water for 8 hours in summer or 20 hours in winter. *Reserve water.* (Soaking water should always be 3 times volume of beans. The better the water, the better the final taste of the tofu.)

•2. After soaking, divide beans and soaking water into several easy-to-handle portions according to the size of your blender. (By volume, the amount of beans to water should be the same. If the amount of soaking water is not sufficient, add water.) Purée each portion for 2 minutes in a blender.

•3. Bring 4 cups water to a boil in a *large* pot and add puréed beans. Bring to a boil over medium heat, stirring continuously to prevent scorching. When foam rises to the top of pot, turn off heat. After foam recedes somewhat, cook for 5 minutes over *very* low heat, stirring constantly.

79

•4. Mix calcium sulfate with 1½ Tbsps water. Stir until powder is *completely* dissolved.

•5. Prepare a cheesecloth-lined colander. Filter liquid through cheesecloth. Pull up ends of cloth, then twist while holding with large tongs (or clean pliers) and squeeze out as much liquid as possible. This liquid is the "soy milk." The material left in the cloth is *okara*, or "tofu pulp." (For recipe using *okara*, see page 86.)

•6. Heat (or cool) soy milk over *low* heat to 165°F (75°C). Keep a careful eye on soy milk and adjust heat to prevent boiling over. Stir once or twice. While soy milk is still circulating, add calcium sulfate mixture in one sweeping circular motion and stir *only* once or twice. *Do not overstir.* Let stand for 10 minutes.

•7. Line a metal colander, wooden tofu box, or 1-quart (1-liter) plastic container that has drainage holes with cheesecloth. (The cheesecloth must be large enough so that it can be folded over to cover coagulating tofu mixture. If using perforated plastic container, prop up both ends to allow quick drainage.) Place in sink or in a pan to catch drainage.

•8. Pour liquid into colander and fold ends of cheesecloth over top. Place a plate on top of cheesecloth (for tofu box use wooden top), and a 2-lb (1-kg) weight on top of the plate (a 2-cup measuring cup filled with water works well). Let stand for 15 to 20 minutes.

•9. Lift tofu out of colander by taking hold of cheesecloth, and lower into a large bowl of cold water. (If using a tofu box, remove bottom and allow tofu to slide into a large bowl of cold water.) Gently unwrap while it is under water.

•10. Soak tofu in cold water for 30 minutes (to remove excess coagulant). Use tofu as desired, or follow the three simple steps in Chilled Fresh Tofu (following recipe) and savor tofu at its freshest.

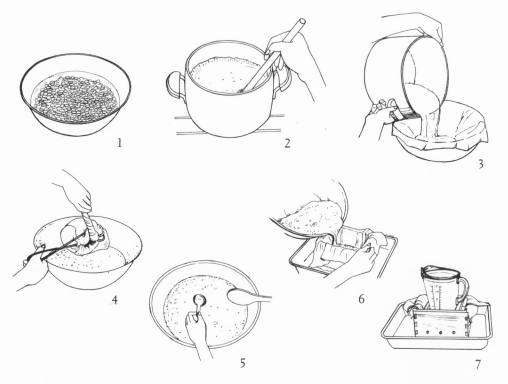

Chilled Fresh Tofu
(Hiyayakko)

Prepare this dish on a hot afternoon when something light and refreshing is called for. Since tofu is at its best the day it is made, use the freshest tofu possible.

SERVES 4   128 Cal. per serving
---

2 cakes tofu, about 10 oz (285 g) each

CONDIMENTS
2 rounded Tbsps finely chopped green onion
1½ inches (4 cm) fresh ginger, finely grated
1 rounded Tbsp loose bonito flakes (*hana-katsuo*)
3–4 Tbsps soy sauce

•1. Cut tofu in half crosswise. Plunge into boiling water for 5 *seconds*, then transfer immediately to large bowl of ice water.

•2. While water is boiling for step 1, prepare CONDIMENTS.

•3. Drain tofu and place 1 piece tofu in each of 4 individual serving bowls. Mound ½ rounded Tbsp green onion and a dab of grated ginger on top of each serving. Top with small pinch bonito flakes. Season with soy sauce to taste (about 1 Tbsp).

Simmered Tofu
(Yudofu)

Simmered Tofu is as popular in winter as Chilled Fresh Tofu is in summer. Like its summer counterpart, Simmered Tofu is served simply and without fanfare, a return to the basic pure taste. Serve at the table in an electric skillet or heat tofu and bring the hot tofu to the table still simmering in kelp stock, keeping dipping sauce hot until ready to serve.

SERVES 4   154 Cal. per serving
---

2 cakes regular tofu, about 10 oz (285 g) each
6-inch (15-cm) piece kelp (*konbu*)
1 tsp cornstarch
pinch salt

CONDIMENTS
1-inch (2½-cm) piece fresh ginger, finely grated
3–4 green onions, finely chopped

DIPPING SAUCE
½ cup loose bonito flakes (*hana-katsuo*), about ⅓ oz (10 g)
7 Tbsps soy sauce
3 Tbsps secondary bonito stock
1 Tbsp *mirin*

•1. Prepare CONDIMENTS.

•2. Combine DIPPING SAUCE ingredients in a saucepan and bring to a boil over medium heat. Boil for 5 *seconds*, then remove from heat. Strain through a cheesecloth-lined wire strainer into a small heat-resistant cup. (A pyrex custard cup is good for this purpose.) Place cup in the middle of electric skillet (or keep sauce hot until ready to serve).

•3. Lightly wipe both sides of kelp with a damp cloth and make ½-inch (1½-cm) cuts with scissors at 1-inch (2½-cm) intervals (see page 35). Cut in half. Place in bottom of medium-sized electric skillet. Add about 3 cups cold water, pinch salt, and cornstarch dissolved in 2 tsps water.

•4. Cut each tofu cake into 8 pieces. Add cut tofu (it should be completely covered by water) and bring to a soft boil over medium heat. When water boils and tofu floats, it is ready. Ladle hot sauce into individual dipping dishes and season with condiments to taste.

Tofu Steak

Blocks of tofu are pan-fried until they are a crisp golden brown, then doused with a soy sauce- and saké-based mixture. Serve hot from the skillet.

SERVES 4	239 Cal. per serving

2 cakes regular tofu, about 10 oz (285 g) each
2 Tbsps soy sauce
3 Tbsps flour
3 Tbsps oil

SAUCE
3 Tbsps soy sauce
2 Tbsps saké
1 Tbsp *mirin*

CONDIMENTS
2 rounded Tbsps finely chopped green onion
4 rounded Tbsps loose bonito flakes (*hana-katsuo*)
1½ inches (4 cm) fresh ginger, finely grated

•1. Wrap each cake of tofu in a cloth and set on a cutting board. Raise one end of cutting board slightly and place a heavy plate or another cutting board on top of tofu to press out excess moisture. Let stand 10 to 15 minutes.

•2. While tofu is draining, prepare CONDIMENTS.

•3. Cut tofu in half crosswise. Sprinkle soy sauce over tofu, turning each piece to coat all sides. Allow any excess soy sauce to drain off. Coat with flour.

•4. Heat oil in a large skillet to medium and cook tofu on top and bottom (on all sides if an extra crunchy exterior is desired) until golden brown. While tofu is cooking, combine SAUCE ingredients. When tofu is done, pour sauce over tofu, then *immediately* remove pan from heat.

•5. Arrange tofu on individual serving dishes with side cooked last face up. Sprinkle on chopped green onion and bonito flakes. Add grated ginger. Spoon some sauce from skillet around (not over) tofu and serve immediately.

Deep-fried Fresh Tofu and Eggplant
(Agedashi-dofu)

Here is a combination of home-style and common-sense cooking in a delightful dish topped with a simple sauce and condiments. It is worth searching for Japanese potato starch. Wholesome and filling.

SERVES 4	243 Cal. per serving

2 cakes regular tofu, about 10 oz (285 g) each
4–5 Tbsps potato starch (*katakuriko*) or cornstarch
1 eggplant, about 10 oz (285 g)
2–3 cups vegetable oil

SAUCE
1 cup secondary bonito stock
¼ cup soy sauce
¼ cup *mirin*

CONDIMENTS
½ cup finely grated daikon radish or white radish or turnip
1 Tbsp finely grated fresh ginger
2 Tbsps finely chopped green onion

•1. Cut each cake of tofu in half lengthwise and then crosswise into thirds. Arrange pieces on a clean kitchen towel atop a cutting board and cover with another towel. Raise one end of chopping board slightly and place a heavy plate or another cutting board on top of tofu to press out excess moisture (see previous recipe). Let stand for 30 minutes. Using a clean cloth, pat tofu dry. Coat tofu pieces in potato starch (or cornstarch).

•2. Cut off cap and quarter eggplant lengthwise. Score skin with a diamond pattern ½ inch (1½ cm) apart. Cut each piece diagonally into 4 pieces. Soak in cold water for 15 to 20 minutes.

•3. Prepare CONDIMENTS.

•4. Heat oil in wok or deep skillet until very hot. Slip in tofu pieces a few at a time and keep separated. When color turns a pale golden brown on all sides, remove tofu pieces to absorbent paper.

•5. Squeeze moisture from eggplant and wipe dry with a cloth. Slide cut side(s) into oil and cook eggplant until soft. Drain, cut side down, on absorbent paper.

•6. Bring SAUCE ingredients to a boil over medium heat and then remove from heat.

•7. In each of 4 small bowls make a pyramid of 3 tofu slices. Arrange pieces of eggplant decoratively alongside tofu. Spoon on 1 Tbsp grated daikon, ¼ Tbsp grated ginger, and ½ Tbsp chopped green onion on top of each pyramid. Add more daikon as desired. Ladle sauce into bowls (not over tofu) and serve.

Grilled Tofu with Three Toppings

(Tofu dengaku)

Three thick miso toppings are spread on cracker-sized pieces of tofu, then broiled till edges are delicately browned. Serve piping hot as a snack, hors d'oeuvre, or side dish. Toppings are also good as dips for fresh vegetables.

SERVES 4	327 Cal. per serving

2 cakes regular tofu, about 10 oz
   (285 g) each
vegetable oil
12 bamboo forks (optional)

TOPPING 1
1 ½ Tbsps black sesame seeds
2 ½ –3 Tbsps red miso
1 ½ Tbsps secondary bonito stock
1–1 ½ Tbsps sugar
1 Tbsp *mirin*

TOPPING 2
2 ½ –3 Tbsps red miso
1 ½ Tbsps secondary bonito stock
1–1 ½ Tbsps sugar
1 Tbsp *mirin*

TOPPING 3
2 ½ –3 Tbsps white miso
1 ½ Tbsps secondary bonito stock
1–1 ½ Tbsps sugar
1 Tbsp *mirin*

•**1.** Cut each cake of tofu crosswise into 6 equal rectangular slices. Arrange slices on a clean kitchen towel atop a cutting board and cover with another towel. Raise one end of chopping board slightly and place a heavy plate or another cutting board on top of tofu to press out excess moisture (see page 82). Let stand for 20 to 30 minutes.

•**2.** Prepare miso toppings.

TOPPING 1 and TOPPING 2: Toast and grind sesame seeds (see page 30) and set aside. Mix all ingredients for both toppings together (excluding sesame seed). Stir constantly over medium heat until mixture thickens and volume is slightly reduced (2–3 minutes). Remove from heat. Divide mixture in half. Add sesame seed to 1 portion.

TOPPING 3: Combine all ingredients. Heat over medium heat, stirring constantly, until mixture thickens and volume is slightly reduced.

•**3.** Preheat oven to 475°F (245°C). Line broiler pan with foil and rub with a little vegetable oil. Arrange tofu slices on broiler pan. Bake until tofu surface browns slightly (about 10 minutes). Remove.

•**4.** Preheat broiler unit. Divide each topping.among 4 tofu slices, spreading 1 heaping tsp on each piece. Broil until edges of topping darken slightly (3–4 minutes). Serve hot from the oven. Before serving, insert bamboo forks for easier handling, if desired.

Freeze-dried Tofu and Shrimp

(Koya-dofu to ebi no nimono)

Here is a simple recipe that introduces freeze-dried tofu, or Koya-dofu (see page 32 for other names), a wonderful protein-rich product that, when reconstituted, is soft and spongy, has a taste all its own, and absorbs flavors admirably. Convenient and nourishing, freeze-dried tofu is a pleasant addition to soups and simmered dishes. Try it in some of your own dishes—it may soon become a household favorite.

SERVES 4

189 Cal. per serving

4 freeze-dried tofu pieces (*Koya-dofu* or *kori-dofu*), 2–3 oz (60–85 g) total
11 oz (315 g) shrimp
7 oz (200 g) okra or green beans
dash *mirin*

INGREDIENTS A
1 egg white
1 Tbsp saké
1½ Tbsps cornstarch
⅓ tsp salt

INGREDIENTS B
2½ cups secondary bonito stock
2 Tbsps sugar
1 Tbsp soy sauce
1 tsp salt

INGREDIENTS C
½ cup secondary bonito stock
2 Tbsps sugar

•1. Soak freeze-dried tofu in warm water until soft (1–2 hours). Weigh down with plate or drop-lid (see page 91) so that tofu is entirely immersed. When soft, rinse in cold water and squeeze out excess water by pressing tofu between palms. Repeat until water no longer comes out milky. Tofu should be spongy. Cut in half crosswise.

•2. Prepare 3 cups bonito stock.

•3. Shell and devein shrimp (see page 38). Roughly chop. Add shrimp and INGREDIENTS A to food processor and whir until smooth paste is formed.

•4. Combine INGREDIENTS B and bring to a boil over medium heat. Reduce to simmer. With moistened tablespoon, drop rounded spoonfuls of shrimp paste into simmering liquid. There should be at least 8 portions. Cook over low heat, rotating shrimp "quenelles" occasionally to cook on all sides. When quenelles float to the top, rotate them. (They will sink slightly.) When they no longer sink when rotated, they are done (2–3 minutes). Remove quenelles from pan and set aside.

•5. Raise to medium heat, add INGREDIENTS C to simmering broth, and bring to a boil. Add tofu and cover with drop-lid and pan lid. Reduce heat to low and simmer until liquid is nearly absorbed. Remove from heat.

•6. Rub okra with salted cloth to remove rough surface (or trim green beans). Lightly cook okra (or green beans) in boiling water until tender-crisp. Drain. Sprinkle with salt and dash *mirin*.

•7. Arrange tofu, shrimp, and vegetable on plate and serve hot or at room temperature.

Okara and Vegetable Mélange
(Iriokara)

A good, economical source of protein, okara—a byproduct of tofu—absorbs flavors well and is often combined with vegetables as is done in this recipe. If you do not make your own tofu (see page 79 for recipe), look for okara at a local fresh tofu outlet (or makers). Though some argue that okara keeps as long as a week refrigerated in its original moist state, flavor and freshness deteriorate after the first day, so it is best to dry the okara by roasting it in an oven or sautéing it (see step 3) and then refrigerating it until ready to use. If frozen, okara keeps 1 month.

SERVES 6   165 Cal. per serving

1 ½ cups fresh *okara* (tofu pulp),
    about 9 oz (250 g)
3 dried *shiitake* mushrooms
3 inches (8 cm) carrot
8 green beans
2 Tbsps oil
4 oz (115 g) ground pork (optional)

SIMMERING LIQUID
1 cup secondary bonito stock
3 Tbsps soy sauce
1 Tbsp sugar
2 Tbsps *mirin*
½ tsp salt

•1. Soak mushrooms in warm water until soft (about 1 hour), keeping them submerged by covering with drop-lid (see page 91), flat pan lid, or saucer.

•2. Peel carrot. Sliver carrots as if sharpening a pencil. Slivers should be thin, irregular, and about 1 inch (2 ½ cm) long. Slice green beans and mushrooms (discard stems) into thin strips.

•3. Place *okara* in colander and rinse under cold running water. Wrap in cheesecloth and squeeze out excess moisture. Sauté in hot oil, *stirring constantly*, until *okara* is dry (about 5 minutes). Remove from heat. (If *okara* is refrigerated at this stage, it keeps 5 to 7 days.)

•4. Combine SIMMERING LIQUID and bring to a boil over medium heat. Add vegetables and ground pork. Cook until vegetables are tender.

•5. Add *okara*. Continue cooking, stirring constantly, until liquid is almost absorbed. Final result should be crumbly and moist. It should not be too dry. Serve at room temperature.

VEGETABLES

Simmered Squash
(Kabocha no nimono)

Economical, nutritious, tasty, and simple—all these aptly describe the following recipe and its two variations, which open a new avenue for squash-lovers. Try acorn squash to start or your own favorite winter squash. Adjust sugar to taste.

SERVES 4   197 Cal. per serving

1½–1¾ lb (685–800 g) winter
   squash (orange or yellow flesh)
1¾ cups secondary bonito stock
   or water

2 Tbsps sugar
2 Tbsps *mirin*
1 tsp salt
1 Tbsp soy sauce

•1. Peel squash (if rind is tough and inedible when cooked) and cut into rough 2-inch (5-cm) square chunks.

•2. In a saucepan combine squash, bonito stock, sugar, *mirin*, and salt. Cover with drop-lid (see page 91) and pan lid and cook over medium heat until tender.

•3. Add soy sauce. Mix by rotating pan. *Do not stir with a utensil.* Continue cooking, uncovered, occasionally rotating pan, until liquid is almost absorbed. Remove from the heat. Cool slightly. Serve hot or at room temperature.

Lemony Squash
(Kabocha no remon-ni)

SERVES 5–6   240 Cal. per serving

2–2¼ lb (about 1 kg) winter
   squash (orange or yellow flesh)
5 Tbsps sugar

½ tsp salt
2 tsps soy sauce
½ lemon, sliced

•1. Peel squash (if rind is tough and inedible when cooked) and cut into rough 2-inch (5-cm) square chunks.

•2. Combine squash, 1¼ cups water, sugar, salt, and soy sauce in a saucepan. Cover with drop-lid (see page 91) and pan lid. Simmer until squash is tender and liquid is nearly absorbed.

•3. Arrange lemon slices over squash, replace pan lid only, remove from heat, and allow to sit 3 or 4 minutes to let lemon flavor blend in. Serve garnished with lemon slices.

Squash and Ground Chicken
(Kabocha to torihikiniku no nimono)

SERVES 5–6   301 Cal. per serving

2–2¼ lb (about 1 kg) winter
   squash (orange or yellow flesh)
5 Tbsps sugar
2 tsps salt

2 tsps soy sauce
½ lb (225 g) ground chicken
1½ Tbsps cornstarch

•1. Prepare squash as directed in Lemony Squash (preceding recipe), using 2 tsps salt and 1 tsp soy sauce. When squash is tender, distribute chicken evenly over the top, sprinkle with remaining soy sauce, and replace pan lid only. Continue cooking until chicken is done (about 3–4 minutes).

•2. Mix cornstarch with 2 Tbsps cold water and sprinkle over liquid (not over squash and chicken). Replace lid and cook over medium heat, shaking pan gently until liquid thickens. Spoon thickened sauce over squash and serve.

Baked Eggplant
(Yakinasu)

Years ago in Japan eggplant was wrapped in a sheet of damp Japanese paper (washi) and baked in the ashes of the hearth fire. Those days are gone, but the combination of oriental condiments has been passed on.

SERVES 4   40 Cal. per serving

2 eggplants, about 10 oz (285 g)
   each
1½ inches (4 cm) fresh ginger,
   finely grated

3–4 rounded Tbsps loose bonito
   flakes (*hana-katsuo*)
3–4 Tbsps soy sauce

•1. Preheat broiler. Wash eggplant and discard any leaves but leave cap intact. Wrap whole eggplant in foil and broil for 15 to 25 minute (depending on size) until eggplant softens. Turn occasionally.

•2. When cool enough to handle, peel eggplant. Place on cutting board, and while holding cap end with one hand, pierce eggplant near cap completely through to cutting board with a skewer and pull towards you to separate eggplant meat into 5 or more strips. Cut off cap and halve eggplant lengthwise.

•3. Make a small mound of grated ginger alongside ½ eggplant. Top eggplant with rounded Tbsp of loose bonito flakes. Sprinkle on soy sauce to taste and serve.

Sesame Eggplant
(Nasu no goma-ni)

Plump eggplant topped with freshly toasted and ground sesame seed always finds eager takers at my table. Deep-frying the eggplant before simmering it in stock improves the flavor and prevents it from becoming soggy when simmered.

SERVES 4	121 Cal. per serving

2 eggplants, about 10 oz (285 g) each
3 Tbsps white sesame seeds
2 cups vegetable oil
1 cup secondary bonito stock

1 ½ Tbsps sugar
1 Tbsp soy sauce
1 ½ tsps cornstarch (optional)

•1. Peel eggplant and quarter lengthwise. Soak in cold water for 15 to 20 minutes. Wrap one piece at a time in a paper towel or absorbent cloth and gently press to remove excess water.

•2. Toast and grind sesame seeds (see page 30).

•3. Heat oil in wok or deep skillet to medium deep-frying temperature (340°F/170°C). Test oil with a small crouton-sized piece of bread. If it rises immediately and browns evenly, then oil is ready. Carefully lay in eggplant and turn frequently until slightly but evenly browned. Drain on absorbent paper to remove excess oil.

•4. Place eggplant in a skillet flat side down. Add just enough bonito stock to cover eggplant. Bring to a boil over medium heat and add sugar. Continue boiling over medium heat for 1 minute, then sprinkle on soy sauce and sesame.

•5. Transfer eggplant to serving platter, spoon on sauce, and serve. For thicker sauce, add cornstarch mixed with 2 tsps cold water and simmer, while mixing, until thickened.

Simmered Chinese Cabbage and Deep-fried Tofu
(Age-dofu hakusai-ni)

Found in the refrigerator section of oriental markets, atsuage *is thick tofu (not thin) that has been deep-fried to a golden brown while the inside remains fresh and tender. It makes a hearty protein source and is often used in soups and simmered dishes.*

14 oz (400 g) Chinese cabbage
2 thick deep-fried tofu (*atsuage*),
   5–7 oz (140–200 g)

SIMMERING LIQUID
1 ⅓ cups secondary bonito stock
2 Tbsps soy sauce
2 Tbsps sugar
2 Tbsps saké

•1. Separate cabbage leaves. Submerge in boiling water to soften slightly. Drain. Cut crosswise into 2-inch (5-cm) wide strips. If the leaves are quite wide, cut in half lengthwise first.

•2. Immerse deep-fried tofu in boiling water for 30 seconds to remove excess oil (or pour boiling water over tofu). Drain. Cut in half crosswise, then cut each piece diagonally in half (into triangles).

•3. In a saucepan combine SIMMERING LIQUID and bring to a boil. Add tofu. Cover with a drop-lid (see page 91) and pan lid, then simmer for 10 minutes.

•4. Turn tofu and push to one side. Add cabbage. Replace both lids and simmer until cabbage is done (about 10 minutes). Serve.

Turnip Cups with Miso Sauce
(Kabu no furofuki)

Filled with a tangy sauce and topped with a decorative cap, turnips are presented in a memorable fashion. This simple, no-fuss dish requires little preparation and is ideal for entertaining on short notice. Small turnips are best. Be sure to check carefully for dirt trapped at base of stems. Keep turnips hot and add sauce just before serving.

SERVES 4   101 Cal. per serving

4 turnips, about 3 oz (85 g) each
6-inch (15-cm) piece kelp (*konbu*)
salt

MISO SAUCE
4 Tbsps red miso
2 Tbsps sugar
3 Tbsps secondary bonito stock
2 Tbsps *mirin*
1 egg yolk
2 tsps fresh ginger juice (see page 27)

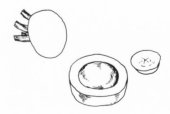

•1. Trim all but ¾ inch (2 cm) of stem from each turnip. Peel. Trim a small piece from bottom of each turnip so that it will stand upright. Cut off the top of each turnip ½ inch (1½ cm) below the stem. This will be the decorative cap.

•2. Lightly wipe both sides of kelp with a damp cloth and make ½-inch (1½-cm) cuts with scissors at 1-inch (2½-cm) intervals (see page 35). Place kelp and turnips (without tops) in a saucepan. Add a pinch salt and enough water to cover turnips. Cover and place over high heat until water comes to a rapid boil. Remove and discard kelp and simmer turnips until *just* tender. Add turnip tops and continue to simmer until turnips and tops are done. (Simmering time varies with size of turnips.)

•3. MISO SAUCE: Meanwhile, combine miso, *mirin*, sugar, and bonito stock in a small saucepan. Stirring constantly, cook over medium heat until mixture thickens and volume is partially reduced. Cool slightly. *Quickly* blend egg yolk and ginger juice into sauce.

DROP-LID (*OTOSHI-BUTA*): This lightweight wooden utensil is employed when simmering foods. The drop-lid is placed directly on top of materials to be cooked (or floats on the surface of the simmering liquid).

It serves several functions, depending on the ingredients it is used with. In general, it shortens the cooking time and assists in flavor penetration. When only a small amount of seasoning or simmering liquid is being used, it ensures even cooking by forcing equal distribution of fluids (or when there is enough liquid, by keeping foods submerged). A drop-lid insulates ingredients and allows for even cooking (without having to turn food) by forcing rising heat back down through the food. The drop-lid is also applied when simmering fragile foods that would otherwise break up from the force of circulating liquid if movement was not minimized. Finally, if placed on exposed surfaces, the drop-lid, in addition to its other functions, keeps food from drying out.

Drop-lids are inexpensive and practical for everyday cooking as well, and, if you can find them, pick up several sizes and keep them on hand. Diameter of drop-lid should be 1 to 2 inches (2½ to 5 cm) smaller than diameter of pot.

Before using a drop-lid, soak it in water for a few minutes until it is saturated. This prevents it from absorbing cooking liquids. Newly purchased drop-lids must be broken in before they can be used. Soak new drop-lids for at least 30 minutes in the milky water obtained from washing rice, or in a solution of water and sodium bicarbonate (baking soda) to remove wood odor.

Wash with mild soap, rinse *well*, and allow to dry completely before storing, unwrapped, in a dry place.

Substitutes: A drop-lid is recommended but not a must. Several options are open: compensate for the lack of a drop-lid by additional stirring, turning, and mixing of ingredients where it is possible to do so or replace it with a similar object. Aluminum plates or pie pans, flat lightweight pan lids, and baking paper are all acceptable alternatives. Cut baking paper slightly larger than pot to be used, make one or two small vents to allow steam to escape, and push it down into the pot so that outer edges bend upward and hold paper in place. Since baking paper will remain stationary, occasionally push it down as level of liquid drops.

•4. When turnips are done, remove from saucepan and drain. With a spoon hollow out enough of each turnip center to hold 2 tsps sauce. Fill each with 2 tsps hot miso sauce. Arrange with turnip top propped against side of filled turnip. Serve immediately.

Stuffed Cabbage, Japanese Style
(Kyabetsu no kenchin-ni)

The Japanese version of this dish is stuffed with puréed and seasoned tofu that has been combined with diced and simmered mushrooms and carrots. An excellent accompaniment to grilled dishes.

SERVES 4	153 Cal. per serving

5 outer cabbage leaves, either round or Chinese cabbage
4 dried *shiitake* mushrooms
2 inches (5 cm) carrot
5 green beans
1 cake regular tofu, about 10 oz (285 g)
1 egg
2 tsps fresh ginger juice (see page 27)
flour
cornstarch
toothpicks

SIMMERING LIQUID A
1 cup secondary bonito stock
2 Tbsps soy sauce
1 Tbsp sugar

TOFU MIXTURE
2 tsps soy sauce
1 tsp sugar
⅓ tsp salt

SIMMERING LIQUID B
2 cups secondary bonito stock
2 Tbsps saké
1 Tbsp soy sauce
1 Tbsp sugar
1 tsp salt

To prepare

•1. Soak mushrooms in warm water until soft (about 1 hour), keeping them submerged by covering with drop-lid (see page 91), flat pan lid, or saucer.

•2. Prepare a total of 3 cups bonito stock.

•3. Blanch 4 cabbage leaves for 1 or 2 minutes in boiling water. (Reserve fifth leaf until later.) Drain and cool. On the outside bottom third of each leaf, pare off a bit of the thick vein in the center to make rolling easier later on. Lightly sprinkle inside surface of leaves with flour.

•4. Drain mushrooms. Peel carrot. Finely dice carrot and mushrooms. Combine with SIMMERING LIQUID A. Simmer until liquid is nearly absorbed. Cool.

•5. Blanch green beans 1 or 2 minutes. Drain and thinly slice diagonally.

•6. Wrap tofu in cheesecloth, twist ends, and gently compress by hand to squeeze out excess moisture. Whir in a blender or food processor for 5 seconds. Add ingredients for TOFU MIXTURE. Whir until a smooth paste is formed (about 5 seconds). Transfer tofu mixture to bowl and stir in *well-drained* carrot, mushrooms, and green beans. Mix in egg.

To cook and serve

•1. Place a portion of tofu mixture in the center of each blanched leaf. Fold bottom of leaf over mixture, then fold sides inward and roll up. Secure with toothpicks.

•2. Place the fifth cabbage leaf on the bottom of saucepan to prevent rolls from sticking. Place cabbage rolls in saucepan, seam side down. Add SIMMERING LIQUID B. Cover with pan lid and simmer over medium heat until liquid is nearly absorbed (about 15 minutes).

•3. Remove cabbage rolls and cool slightly. Serve whole or cut into 1½-inch (4-cm) pieces. Arrange cut side up on a small serving platter. To remaining liquid in the pan, add small amount of cornstarch mixed with water. Stir over medium heat until liquid thickens. Spoon a little sauce over cabbage rolls. Sprinkle on ginger juice and serve.

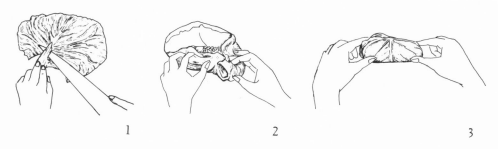

1　　　　　　　　　2　　　　　　　　　3

Simmered Soybeans and Vegetables
(Gomoku nimame)

Soybeans, an excellent protein source, have no cholesterol and very little saturated fat. One cup cooked soybeans is equal in protein to a 5-ounce (140-gram) steak. Traditionally, simmered beans is a sweet dish in Japan. You may want to adjust sugar.

SERVES 4　　　　　　　　　　　　　　　　551 Cal. per serving

1½ cups dried soybeans
2 dried *shiitake* mushrooms
6-inch (15-cm) piece kelp (*konbu*)
3 oz (85 g) canned bamboo shoots

4 inches (10 cm) carrot
1 cup light brown sugar
5 Tbsps soy sauce

•1. Wash and sort beans. Soak overnight in 5 cups water.

•2. Soak mushrooms in warm water until soft (about 1 hour), keeping them submerged by covering with drop-lid (see page 91), flat pan lid, or saucer.

•3. Transfer beans and soaking water to a pressure cooker, bring to full pressure, and cook for 20 minutes over a *very* low heat. (If using ordinary saucepan, bring to a boil, reduce to simmer, and cook for 1 hour, making sure beans are always covered with water.)

•4. Drain mushrooms and discard stems. Chop mushrooms, kelp (lightly wipe both sides with a damp cloth), bamboo shoots, and carrot into pieces the size of soybeans.

•5. Place soybeans, vegetables, half of sugar, and enough water from cooking soybeans to cover in a saucepan. Cover with drop-lid and pan lid, and cook over medium heat for 10 minutes.

•6. Dissolve remaining sugar and stir, then add 2½ Tbsps soy sauce. Simmer, uncovered, again until liquid is nearly absorbed. Add remaining soy sauce and simmer over a *very* low heat until liquid is absorbed. Do not let beans dry out. Serve hot or at room temperature.

Tofu and Vegetable Squares
(Gisei-dofu)

High in protein, tofu squares with their rich combination of egg, tofu, and tender-crisp vegetables are popular among children at mealtime and as snacks.

SERVES 4   150 Cal. per serving

1½ cakes regular tofu, about
   15 oz (425 g) total
2 dried *shiitake* mushrooms
3 inches (8 cm) carrot

3 green beans
2 eggs
2 Tbsps sugar
3 Tbsps soy sauce

To prepare

•1. Soak mushrooms in warm water until soft (about 1 hour), keeping them submerged by covering with drop-lid (see page 91), flat pan lid, or saucer.

•2. Mash tofu well by hand. Drain mushrooms and discard stems. Peel carrot. Finely chop carrot and mushrooms. Slice green beans diagonally into thin strips.

•3. Parboil vegetables together (including mushrooms).

•4. Prepare a cheesecloth-lined colander. Add mashed tofu to parboiled vegetables, stir once or twice, then pour vegetable and tofu mixture into a cheesecloth-lined colander. Draw cloth up around mixture and twist ends to remove most, but not all, of the moisture.

•5. Beat eggs and combine with mixture in a bowl. Add sugar, soy sauce, and pinch salt.

To cook and serve

•1. Preheat a 9-inch (23-cm) skillet over low heat. Lightly oil bottom and sides of skillet. Reheat. Pour in mixture in an even layer and cook over low heat. Pierce through to bottom of skillet in several places to allow even heat distribution. Turn when bottom of tofu patty is firmly cooked and slightly browned. Cook until second side is also firm and slightly browned.

•2. Turn out onto cutting board. Cut into 8 equal pieces. Serve hot or cold. Keeps 2 days at most.

SALADS

Tuna and Cucumber with Sweet Vinegar Dressing
(Tsuna to kyuri no sunomono)

More accurately this dish and those to follow should be called either "vinegared foods" or "dressed foods." Often served in minute portions as a prelude to the meal, a little goes a long way, so the portions are small but provocative. A variety of dressings are presented in these recipes, and they all are easily adapted to individual taste. Try some of these dressings on your own salads or vegetable combinations. Sweet vinegar dressing keeps 1 week covered and refrigerated.

SERVES 4	148 Cal. per serving

¾ lb (340 g) cucumber
6 oz (170 g) canned tuna packed in oil
1 tsp rice vinegar
1 Tbsp finely slivered fresh ginger

SWEET VINEGAR DRESSING
3 Tbsps rice vinegar
1 Tbsp sugar
1 tsp soy sauce
¼ tsp salt

•1. Peel and seed cucumber. Thinly slice crosswise. Sprinkle with salt and set aside. Cut ginger into extremely fine slivers and soak in water until ready to use.

•2. Combine SWEET VINEGAR DRESSING ingredients. Drain tuna and reserve oil.

•3. Squeeze out excess moisture from cucumber by hand (or use cheesecloth). Rinse quickly, then squeeze again. Sprinkle with rice vinegar.

•4. Combine cucumber and dressing. Gently mix in tuna. Pour in tuna oil and mix thoroughly.

•5. Drain ginger. Mound salad in small bowls and sprinkle with ginger slivers.

VARIATIONS: Boiled chicken, cooked fish, or shellfish can be used in place of tuna.

Crab and Cucumber with Golden Dressing
(Kani to kyuri no kimizu-ae)

Golden dressing is nearly the same consistency as fresh mayonnaise but without the oil. Lightly vinegared, it is the perfect topping for crisp cucumber and sweet crab meat. Of course, fresh boiled or steamed crab meat can be used, if desired. Dressing keeps 1 week covered and refrigerated.

SERVES 4	85 Cal. per serving

6 oz (170 g) canned crab meat
1 small cucumber
rice vinegar

GOLDEN DRESSING

2 egg yolks	1 Tbsp sugar
4 Tbsps secondary bonito stock	¾ tsp cornstarch
2 Tbsps rice vinegar	⅔ tsp salt

•1. Peel and seed cucumber. Slice thinly crosswise. Soak for 10 minutes in 1 cup water containing scant ½ tsp salt.

•2. Drain crab meat. Remove any shell or cartilage. Sprinkle lightly with rice vinegar and pinch sugar.

•3. GOLDEN DRESSING: Combine dressing ingredients in a double boiler. Stir constantly over boiling water until mixture thickens. Remove from heat and continue stirring until mixture cools. When dressing approaches a mayonnaise-like consistency, set aside.

•4. Drain cucumber. Wrap in cheesecloth and gently squeeze to remove excess moisture (or squeeze by hand). Lightly sprinkle with rice vinegar.

•5. Mound cucumber in 4 small bowls. Arrange crab alongside cucumber. Spoon 1 Tbsp dressing over each serving.

Fresh Tuna and Green Onion with Miso and Vinegar Dressing
(Negi to maguro no nuta)

Green onion, fresh shellfish, vinegared fish, and other vegetables are nicely complemented with this dressing. If you do not have white miso on hand, increase the sugar slightly and use red miso. As with sashimi, use only the freshest tuna. Dressing keeps 1 week covered and refrigerated.

SERVES 4	148 Cal. per serving

5–7 oz (140–200 g) fresh or frozen raw tuna fillet of sashimi quality	½ tsp *wasabi* horseradish
	2 tsps soy sauce
6–7 mild green onions	2 tsps rice vinegar

4 Tbsps white miso	2–3 Tbsps rice vinegar
2 Tbsps secondary bonito stock	1 tsp hot yellow Japanese mustard
1 Tbsp sugar	(*karashi*) or any hot mustard that
1 Tbsp *mirin*	is not sweet or vinegary

•1. Immerse white end of green onion into boiling salted water until it softens (about 1 minute). Immerse whole onion and parboil. Transfer immediately to cold water and quickly cool. Drain. Arrange onion side by side on a cutting board. Remove the bitter substance from the middle of the onion by running the side of a knife over onion, forcing the substance out at the top. Cut green onion into 1-inch (2½-cm) pieces. Sprinkle with 2 tsps rice vinegar.

•2. Cut tuna into bite-sized cubes. Combine with *wasabi* horseradish and soy sauce and coat well.

•3. MISO AND VINEGAR DRESSING: In a small saucepan combine miso, bonito stock, sugar, and *mirin*. Stir over medium-high heat until mixture reaches boiling point. Remove from heat and let cool. When cool, add rice vinegar and mustard.

•4. Squeeze out any excess moisture from onion. Combine onion, tuna, and dressing. Arrange and serve.

Dressed Spinach
(Horenso no ohitashi)

Soaked in a seasoned stock after boiling, this dish has long been a favorite, perhaps because of its simple, natural taste. Substitute young asparagus, green beans, watercress, or any mild green vegetable. The secret is to drain vegetables well so water does not dilute the light seasoning. Goes well with most dishes.

SERVES 4	36 Cal. per serving
9–11 oz (250–315 g) fresh young spinach, untrimmed	SEASONING
1 tsp soy sauce	½ cup secondary bonito stock
1 rounded Tbsp loose bonito flakes (*hana-katsuo*)	2 Tbsps soy sauce
	1 tsp *mirin*
	pinch salt

•1. Wash spinach well to remove any trapped dirt. Do not trim. Add pinch sugar to a pot with ample amount of boiling water. Soften stems by placing spinach into pot root end first, keeping spinach in a bunch. Spinach bunch should slide into pot on its own accord (give it a helping hand, if necessary). Cook until leaves are *just* tender. Do not overcook. Transfer spinach immediately to a pan of cold water and rinse under cold running water.

•2. Remove excess moisture by holding spinach vertically, root end up, and gently squeezing moisture from spinach by running hand down the length of the flaccid bunch. Sprinkle with 1 tsp soy sauce and again squeeze out moisture in the same manner.

•3. Combine SEASONING ingredients. Place spinach in a small, shallow pan and pour seasoning over spinach. Let stand for 10 minutes. Turn once.

•4. Squeeze out excess seasoning and reserve. Trim about 1 inch (2½ cm) from root end and discard. Reverse the direction of half the bunch and squeeze out any remaining moisture.

•5. Cut crosswise into 1½ - to 2-inch (4- to 5-cm) bundles. Stand each small bundle on end and place in small bowls. Spoon 1½ Tbsps seasoning over each portion. Sprinkle each with small pinch bonito flakes and serve.

Green Beans with Sesame Dressing
(Ingen no goma-ae)

This nutty and aromatic dressing perks up this usually dull but nutritious vegetable. Any green-leafed vegetable such as spinach goes well with this dressing. Toasted almonds, walnuts, and peanuts are delightful alternatives to sesame seeds. Dressing keeps 10 days covered and refrigerated.

SERVES 4	85 Cal. per serving

½ lb (225 g) fresh green beans
mirin

SESAME DRESSING

4 Tbsps white sesame seeds	1 Tbsp sugar (or to taste)
1½ Tbsps secondary bonito stock	1 Tbsp soy sauce

•1. SESAME DRESSING: Toast and grind sesame seeds (see page 30). When seeds have been ground into a rough paste, mix in remaining ingredients. If desired, save 1 tsp unground sesame seeds to sprinkle on as garnish.

•2. Wash and trim green beans. Cut diagonally in half. Cook in salted water until tender-crisp. Drain and sprinkle with *mirin* and salt. Cool.

•3. Mix green beans and dressing thoroughly and serve in a single bowl or in individual small bowls.

Five Vegetables with Tofu Dressing
(Gomoku shira-ae)

Creamy tofu dressing accented with freshly toasted sesame naturally makes this salad popular. Vegetables and dressing can be prepared ahead of time, but do not prepare apple or mix in dressing until ready to serve. Tofu dressing keeps 1 day refrigerated if tofu is very fresh.

3 dried *shiitake* mushrooms
4 inches (10 cm) carrot
½ cucumber
10 green beans
1 sheet thin deep-fried tofu
  (*aburage*), about ⅔ oz (20 g),
  or 1 small red apple
1½–2 cups water or secondary
  bonito stock
2 tsps sugar
1 Tbsp soy sauce

TOFU DRESSING
1 cake regular tofu, 10 oz (285 g)
3 Tbsps white sesame seeds
2 Tbsps sugar
1 tsp salt
¼ tsp soy sauce (optional)

•1. Soak mushrooms in warm water until soft (about 1 hour), keeping them submerged by covering with drop-lid (see page 91), flat pan lid, or saucer. Drain. Discard stems and cut caps into strips ¼ inch (¾ cm) wide.

•2. Peel carrot and cucumber. Cut into rectangular strips 1½ × ½ × ⅛ inches (4 × 1½ × ½ cm). Cut whole green beans in half.

•3. Place *aburage* in colander and rinse with boiling water. Cut *aburage* in half lengthwise, stack halves, then cut crosswise into strips ¼ inch (¾ cm) wide. (See step 8 for apple.)

•4. Combine green beans, *aburage*, mushrooms, and carrot in a medium-sized saucepan. Barely cover with water (or bonito stock). Add sugar and soy sauce. Boil gently over medium heat until liquid is nearly absorbed and vegetables are tender (10–12 minutes) but not soggy. (Except *aburage*, which will be soggy.) Cool.

•5. Sprinkle cucumber lightly with salt and mix by hand. Set aside until cucumber softens. Squeeze out excess liquid by hand or with cheesecloth.

•6. Slip whole tofu cake into a pot of boiling water for 5 or 6 seconds, then immediately transfer to a square of cheesecloth in a colander. Bring cheesecloth around tofu and twist ends gently to squeeze out as much liquid as possible.

•7. TOFU DRESSING: Toast and grind sesame seeds (see page 30). Purée tofu in a blender or food processor until creamy. Add remaining dressing ingredients. Blend until thick and creamy (about 1 minute in processor).

•8. Wash and core apple, then slice into thin strips.

•9. Combine dressing, vegetables, drained cucumber, and *aburage* (or apple). Mix well and serve.

Japanese-style Salad
(Nihon fu sarada)

Chock full of tantalizing bits of crab, saké-seasoned chicken, and fresh vegetables, this salad offers a variety of tastes with every bite. Make the dressing as peppy or as mild as you want by adjusting the amounts of garlic and pepper. Dressing keeps 1 week covered and refrigerated.

SERVES 4   193 Cal. per serving

4 oz (115 g) boned wicken breast
   without skin
3 Tbsps saké
6 oz (170 g) canned crab meat
2 oz (60 g) dried *wakame* seaweed
   (optional)
½ cucumber
4 inches (10 cm) carrot
1 leek
lettuce leaves (optional garnish)
rice vinegar

SESAME DRESSING

4 Tbsps white sesame seeds

3 Tbsps secondary bonito stock

1 Tbsp mayonnaise or ½ Tbsp
   white miso and 1 tsp sugar

5 Tbsps rice vinegar

1 Tbsp soy sauce

2 tsps sugar

1 tsp salt

⅓ tsp finely grated fresh garlic
   seven-spice mixture (*shichimi*) or
   ground red pepper (optional)

•1. Prepare chicken breasts as directed in Chilled *Somen* Noodles (page 114). Drain crab meat. Remove any shell or cartilage.

•2. Soak *wakame* seaweed for 10 minutes in water. Do not soak too long. Rinse. Pour boiling water over *wakame*, then drain and squeeze out excess moisture. Trim away any tough portions and discard. Cut *wakame* into 2-inch (5-cm) lengths. Sprinkle with rice vinegar, and drain again.

•3. Peel and seed cucumber. Peel carrot. Cut cucumber and carrot into thin slivers. Cut leek into 1 ½ -inch (4-cm) lengths, then halve lengthwise and slice thinly. Soak each vegetable separately in cold water until ready to use.

•4. SESAME DRESSING: Toast and grind sesame seeds (see page 30). Add bonito stock and mayonnaise and mix well. Add remaining ingredients (including seven-spice mixture or red pepper to taste, if desired) and mix thoroughly.

•5. Place custard cup filled with dressing in the center of a large round platter. Lay lettuce leaves around dressing. Arrange separate mounds of crab, chicken, *wakame*, leek, carrot, and cucumber on the lettuce.

RICE

Chicken and Egg on Rice
(Oyako donburi)

The literal translation of this dish is "parent-and-child bowl." This hot and wholesome meal-in-a-bowl is perfect with fresh or leftover chicken. Try other leftover meats. For a quick and satisfying meal, combine chicken, egg, and onions. Put mushrooms in water to soak, then begin preparing rice.

SERVES 4	669 Cal. per serving

½ lb (225 g) boned chicken breast
  with or without skin
4 dried *shiitake* mushrooms
2½ cups short-grain rice
12–16 snow peas
4 oz (115 g) canned bamboo shoots
1 onion
4 eggs
½ sheet *nori* seaweed, toasted

SAUCE
1¼ cups secondary bonito stock
4 Tbsps saké
4 Tbsps soy sauce
2 Tbsps sugar

To make plain rice

All recipes call for short-grain rice. When planning a meal requiring rice, allow at least 1 hour for washing, soaking, boiling, and standing. Use a heavy, tight-lidded pot with a capacity roughly 3 times the volume of uncooked rice. (Pot should not be too large for amount of rice to be cooked.) Wash and soak rice in the pot the rice is to be cooked in (or, if you have a rice cooker, in the removable inner tub).

Rice that has been sitting on the shelf will dry out and will absorb more water when boiled than newly harvested rice. For older, drier rice increase amount of water by 20 or 30 percent. In general, if rice comes out drier than expected, increase amount of water by 10 percent increments until desired result is achieved.

•1. *Washing*: Cover rice with cold water and gently stir with your hand until water becomes milky. Do not use so little water that you "grind" the rice. Pour off water, add fresh water, and stir. Repeat until water is *almost* clear. This might take as long as 5 minutes in some cases.

•2. *Soaking*: Add 1.1 cups water for each cup rice. (For older, drier rice increase amount of water by 20 to 30 percent.) Soak for 30 minutes. Soak longer in winter,

101

if desired, but no more than 1 hour. Rice will expand slightly and change from a dull translucent yellow to an almost pure white.

•3. *Boiling*: Bring rice quickly to a boil. Continue to boil for 30 *seconds*, then reduce heat to low, cover, and cook for 12 or 13 minutes. Turn heat to high for 5 seconds, then turn off and remove pot from heat.

During cooking, the lid might clatter from the pressure exerted by escaping steam, and a starchy foam will begin seeping out around the edges. This is as it should be. *Do not lift the lid* during cooking unless water boils over. If this happens, lift lid *slightly* until water level recedes, then adjust heat.

•4. *Standing and fluffing*: *Without lifting or removing lid*, let rice stand for 10 to 15 minutes. This allows rice to absorb the remaining moisture and finish cooking. The rice is not done until *after* it has been allowed to stand untouched. Before serving, gently fluff rice with a wooden spoon (or rice paddle).

To make Chicken and Egg on Rice

•1. Soak mushrooms in warm water until soft (about 1 hour), keeping them submerged by covering with drop-lid (see page 91), flat pan lid, or saucer. Drain well and discard stems. Cut caps into thin strips. (While mushrooms are soaking, begin preparing rice.)

•2. *Snow peas*: Remove stem and strings and trim ends. Slice lengthwise into thin strips. Blanch in boiling water for a few seconds. Drain.
Bamboo: Wash well and remove any white residue. Slice into julienne strips.
Onion: Cut in half and slice thinly.
Chicken: Cut into bite-sized pieces.

•3. Combine SAUCE ingredients and bring to a boil over medium heat. Add onions and chicken. Raise to medium-high heat and cook chicken, turning occasionally. When chicken has lost its pink color, add bamboo and mushroom and cook until chicken is done and vegetables are tender-crisp.

•4. Beat eggs, frothing as little as possible. When vegetables are tender-crisp, pour in egg in a slow, circular motion (covering as much surface area as possible), sprinkle with snow peas, and continue cooking for 30 seconds until egg is *barely* set. (Since hot rice will cook egg even more, leave the egg slightly runny.) Do not stir. Let egg spread by itself.

•5. To serve, divide hot cooked rice among 4 large, deep bowls (about 1½ cups rice per serving). Gently lay chicken and egg on top of rice and add sauce. Top with a sprinkling of toasted *nori* seaweed. (If *nori* has not been pretoasted, toast by lightly passing shiny side over an open flame several times to remove moisture and bring out flavor. Cut into fine shreds with scissors or wrap in a dry cloth and crumble into small pieces.) Serve immediately.

Pork Cutlet on Rice
(Katsudon)

Another meal-in-a-bowl, this dish calls for deep-fried, breaded pork cutlets. The secret to success here, as in Chicken and Egg on Rice, lies in remembering that the egg will be further cooked by the hot rice, so undercook the egg initially.

4 slices pork tenderloin, about
   4 oz (115 g) each
vegetable oil for deep-frying
2½ cups short-grain rice
2 onions
12 snow peas
4 eggs (1 egg per serving)
½ sheet *nori* seaweed, toasted

BREADING
flour
1 egg
1 cup dry bread crumbs

SAUCE (SERVES 4)
1¼ cups secondary bonito stock
5 Tbsps saké
2 Tbsps soy sauce
2 Tbsps sugar

SAUCE (SERVES 1)
5 Tbsps secondary bonito stock
2 tsps saké
½ Tbsp soy sauce
½ Tbsp sugar

•1. Prepare plain rice (see page 101).

•2. Remove stem and strings from snow peas and blanch peas. Slice lengthwise into thin strips. Cut onions in half and slice thinly.

•3. Pound pork with tenderizing mallet. Coat with flour, dip into beaten egg, then coat well with bread crumbs. Deep-fry at medium temperature (340°F/170°C) until golden on both sides. Drain on absorbent paper. Cut crosswise into ½ -inch (1½ -cm) wide slices, keeping slices of each cutlet neatly together.

•4. Combine SAUCE ingredients and ½ sliced onion per serving. Bring to a boil over medium heat and add 1 or 2 cutlets, keeping slices together. (To cook 2 cutlets at once, use a large saucepan in order to allow egg to spread.) Cook until pork is heated through (about 1 minute). Beat eggs (1 egg per serving), frothing as little as possible. Pour egg over and around cutlet in a slow, circular motion (covering as much surface area as possible), sprinkle with snow peas, and continue cooking for 30 seconds until egg is *barely* set. (Since hot rice will cook egg even more, leave the egg slightly runny.) Do not stir. Let egg spread by itself.

•5. Divide hot cooked rice among 4 large, deep bowls (about 1½ cups cooked rice per serving). Carefully lift out 1 pork cutlet, keeping slices neatly together, and place on top of rice. Add egg and vegetable to each bowl, cook remaining cutlets in same manner, then distribute remaining sauce. If *nori* seaweed has not been pretoasted, toast by lightly passing shiny side over an open flame several times. Cut with a scissors into shreds or wrap in a dry cloth and crumble by hand. Sprinkle over pork. Serve immediately.

Tempura on Rice
(Tendon)

Tempura enthusiasts welcome this dish, which combines tempura with the concept of donburi *(a large bowl of rice with tasty toppings) for a hearty home-style meal-in-a-bowl. Like the two preceding dishes,* Tempura on Rice *makes a superb hot lunch, dinner, or late-night snack. Try the mixed-ingredient tempura, instead of shrimp (see variation, page 141).*

SERVES 4   626 Cal. per serving

2 cups short-grain rice
4 large shrimp
1 squid or any small white-fleshed
   fish, about 6 oz (170 g) total
1 bell pepper
vegetable (or tempura) oil for
   deep-frying

SAUCE
1 cup secondary bonito stock
½ cup soy sauce
1 ½–2 Tbsps sugar

BATTER
½–1 egg
½ cup ice water
1 cup sifted flour

•1. Cook plain rice (see page 101).

•2. Clean and cut shrimp, squid (or fish), and bell pepper for deep-frying (see page 139). When rice is almost ready, begin deep-frying tempura. Mix BATTER just before frying.

•3. Combine SAUCE ingredients and bring to a boil over medium heat.

•4. Divide hot cooked rice among 4 bowls (about 1 cup cooked rice per serving). Dip tempura in hot sauce, then arrange on rice. Spoon 1 Tbsp sauce over rice and tempura and serve.

Green Pea Rice
(Aomame gohan)

Fresh or frozen peas work equally well in this dish, which is associated with the coming of spring. Try it with your favorite meat or fish entrée.

SERVES 4   484 Cal. per serving

1 ½ cups tender green peas
2 ½ cups short-grain rice
6-inch (15-cm) piece kelp (*konbu*)
2 Tbsps saké
2 tsps salt

•1. Wash rice (see page 101) 1 hour before boiling. Lightly wipe both sides of kelp with a damp cloth and make ½-inch (1 ½-cm) cuts with scissors at 1-inch (2 ½-cm) intervals (see page 35). Drain rice, then soak in proper amount of cooking water (page 101) with kelp for 30 to 60 minutes.

•2. In a medium-sized *heavy* saucepan combine rice, cooking water, and remaining ingredients. Cover and bring to a boil over high heat. Remove kelp, replace lid, and continue boiling for 30 seconds. Reduce heat to low and boil in same manner as plain rice (page 102).

•3. *Without removing lid*, wait 10 to 15 minutes before serving. Fluff rice and serve in a large bowl.

Mixed Rice
(Gomoku gohan)

In this dish the variety of ingredients gives the rice a rich flavor. Unlike plain rice, which is boiled in water, the rice in this dish is cooked in pot liquor left over from simmering chicken and vegetables. Substitute clams, fish, or meat for chicken. Be sure to try the crispy "scorched" version (see note) if you enjoy crunchy foods.

SERVES 4   632 Cal. per serving

2½ cups short-grain rice
3 dried *shiitake* mushrooms
1 sheet thin deep-fried tofu
  (*aburage*; if available), about
  ⅔ oz (20 g)
5 inches (13 cm) burdock or 3 oz
  (85 g) canned bamboo shoots
5–6 green beans
4 inches (10 cm) carrot
4 oz (115 g) ground chicken
2 Tbsps oil
1 tsp salt

SIMMERING LIQUID
1 cup soaking water from
  mushrooms or secondary bonito
  stock
3 Tbsps saké
1½ Tbsps sugar
2 Tbsps soy sauce

To prepare

•1. Wash mushrooms. Soak in 3 cups warm water until soft (about 1 hour), keeping them submerged by covering with drop-lid (see page 91), flat pan lid, or saucer. Drain, reserving soaking water. Discard stems and cut caps into slices ¼ inch (¾ cm) wide.

•2. Wash rice (see page 101). Cover with damp cloth and drain for 1 hour. While rice is draining, prepare and simmer remaining ingredients. Rice will be cooked in liquid left over from simmered chicken and vegetables (plus soaking water from mushrooms or secondary bonito stock).

•3. Drop sheet of deep-fried tofu into boiling water for 30 seconds, turning once. Rinse in cold water and drain. Trim ¼ inch (¾ cm) from all 4 sides and cut trimmings into 1-inch (2½-cm) lengths. Cut sheet crosswise into thirds. Stack and cut crosswise into ¼-inch (¾-cm) wide strips.

•4. Scrub burdock well with stiff brush under running water, but do not scrape or peel. Score skin lengthwise with the tip of a knife. Sliver burdock as if sharpening a pencil. Burdock slivers should be thin, irregular, and about 1 inch (2½ cm) long. Soak in cold water until ready to use.

•5. Wash and parboil green beans. Slice diagonally into thin strips. Peel carrot. Wash bamboo shoots well and remove any white residue. Cut carrot and bamboo into 1-inch (2½-cm) long julienne strips.

To cook and serve

•1. Sauté ground chicken in oil in a large saucepan until it loses its pink color.

•2. Drain burdock well and add to chicken. Stir. Add carrot, bamboo shoot, deep-fried tofu, and mushroom. (Reserve green beans until next step.) Sauté over medium-high heat until tender-crisp.

•3. Combine SIMMERING LIQUID and add to chicken, tofu, and vegetables (excluding green beans). Cover and simmer for 8 minutes. Add green beans and simmer 1 or 2 minutes. Drain immediately, reserving pot liquor.

•4. Combine pot liquor with enough soaking water from mushrooms (or secondary bonito stock) to make 2¾ cups. Add to saucepan along with rice and salt. Stir. Cover and bring to a boil over medium-high heat. Let it boil 30 seconds, then reduce to low and boil for 12 minutes in same manner as plain rice (see page 102). (If using rice cooker, add liquid, rice, and salt and switch on.)

•5. After rice is done *boiling*, lay vegetables and chicken on top of rice. Do not mix. Replace lid and cook for 2 minutes. Turn heat to high for 5 seconds, then turn off. *Without uncovering*, let stand for 10 to 15 minutes. Mix just before serving. (If using a rice cooker, add cooked vegetables and chicken on top of cooked rice as soon as indicator light goes off. Replace lid and let stand for 10 to 15 minutes, then mix and serve.)

NOTE: An alternate method allows rice and vegetables to be mixed together from the first: Soak mushrooms. Combine simmering ingredients and enough water from soaking mushrooms to make 2¾ cups. Add liquid, raw vegetables, and salt to rice. Cook in a rice cooker or pot in same manner as plain rice. The rice and vegetables will scorch easily if this method is used and so must be watched carefully. Many people, however, prefer this crispy, slightly browned mixed rice. Without removing lid, let stand 10 to 15 minutes before mixing and serving.

Rice Balls
(Onigiri)

Although Onigiri *is almost universally translated as "Rice Balls," shapes are rarely spherical. Rice balls of any shape are tasty and portable fare for a picnic or outing. Since there are no distinguishable outer markings, the cook, by choosing at least two of the three fillings below, can create a curiosity and anticipation as to which filling is hidden inside. This dish takes the place of rice at mealtime, and toasted leftovers make an excellent snack.*

SERVES 4   613 Cal. per serving

3½ cups short-grain rice
1 sheet *nori* seaweed, toasted

FILLINGS
3 oz (85 g) fresh salmon
2 tsps saké
3 rounded Tbsps loose bonito
   flakes (*hana-katsuo*)

2 tsps soy sauce
2 medium pickled plums
   (*umeboshi*) or 1 large pickled
   plum

To prepare
•1. Cook plain rice (see page 101).

•2. While rice is cooking prepare fillings.

Salmon: Broil salmon until lightly browned. Remove bones and skin. Sprinkle with saké. Use about 2 tsps per rice ball.

Bonito: Moisten bonito flakes with soy sauce. Use ½ tsp per rice ball.

Plum: Squeeze out pits from pickled plums. Use 1 plum per rice ball. Cut large plums in half and use half a plum per rice ball.

NOTE: If using only one filling, prepare 6 oz (170 g) salmon, ½ cup loose bonito flakes, or 8 to 10 medium pickled plums (or 4 to 5 large plums).

•3. If *nori* seaweed has not been pretoasted, toast by passing shiny side over an open flame several times. Cut into 1-×-3-inch (2½-×-8-cm) strips.

To form rice balls

•1. Turn hot rice into a large bowl, but do not pack down. (Rice balls are made while rice is hot, but can be eaten hot or at room temperature.)

•2. With a wooden spoon or rice paddle, scoop up about ½ cup unpacked rice and place it in a small bowl or coffee cup. Do not pack down. (This simple step will cool outer rice enough so that it may be handled without difficulty.)

•3. Moisten hands with lightly salted water. (This also seasons rice.) Take ½ cup rice (or an amount you are comfortable with) in cupped fingers of your left hand (if you are right-handed). Make a slight indentation in middle of the rice and add one filling. Close rice over filling.

•4. Use fingers of your right hand to shape into a rough triangle. (Fillings should be in center.) When necessary, rotate by tossing rice lightly in cupped hands to form corners and edges. Avoid packing rice so hard that it is mashed or so loose that "ball" falls apart. Finished triangle should be about 2½ inches (6½ cm) high and 1 inch (2½ cm) thick. Wrap with *nori* seaweed as shown.

VARIATIONS: Triangular rice balls are more impressive, but easier-to-form shapes such as cylinder and "flattened ball" are also common. To make these, simply take ½ cup hot rice, add filling, and shape, following the general principles in recipe.

Rice balls without filling can be made more appetizing by wrapping ball with 2 pieces of *nori* seaweed, each about 3 inches (8 cm) square.

Broiled rice balls, another variation, can be made by forming rice into a flattened ball, brushing with a mixture of 1 Tbsp soy sauce and 2 tsps *mirin*, then broiling in oven or toaster oven until each side is lightly toasted. These are best eaten while hot.

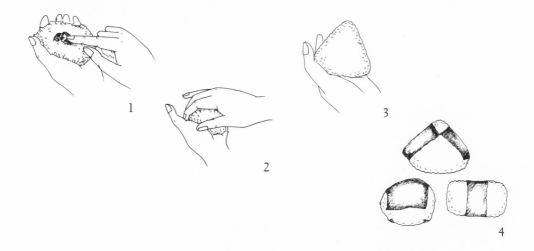

NOODLES

Homemade *Udon* or *Soba* Noodles
(Teuchi udon *or* soba)

Noodle-lovers the world over always appreciate the fresh homemade version, and in Japan they flock to shops where the dough is made fresh daily. Cooking instructions apply to homemade and store-bought noodles.

SERVES 4–5

5 cups all-purpose flour (*udon*)
or
4 cups buckwheat flour and 1 cup all-
    purpose flour (*soba*)
4 tsps salt dissolved in 1 cup water
2 large heavy-gauge plastic bags (see
    step 1)

To make noodles
•1. To flour in a large bowl, add salted water a little at a time and knead by hand until dough sticks together. (If making *soba* noodles, dissolve salt in ½ cup hot water, add to buckwheat flour, knead with plastic spatula, add ½ cup cold water little by little while kneading, and add remaining flour.) Dough will not be completely smooth. Wrap dough in plastic bags, place dough on the floor, and knead with bare feet by stepping back and forth on dough. When dough has been flattened to about 1 foot (30 cm) in diameter, remove from plastic, fold into quarters (wedge-shaped), rewrap in plastic, and resume kneading by foot. Repeat 5 or 6 times until dough is smooth and well mixed. Remove from plastic and wrap dough in a damp cloth for at least 1 hour; it is best, however, to let it stand 3 hours in summer or 6 hours in winter. Do not refrigerate. (If making *soba* noodles, proceed to step 2 without letting dough stand.)
•2. Fold dough into a rectangle approximately 6 × 10 inches (15 × 25 cm). Lightly sprinkle a large work surface with flour to prevent sticking. Roll out dough in all directions, turning over occasionally, and sprinkle with a small amount of flour when necessary to prevent sticking. In order to spread out dough it may be necessary to occasionally fold dough in thirds (use a little flour to prevent sticking) and press down crosswise with rolling pin to "stretch" dough, starting from

the center and working your way towards one end, then returning to center and working your way towards other end.

When dough is about ⅛ inch (½ cm) thick (thinner for *soba* noodles) and about 1½ × 2½ feet (45 × 75 cm), sprinkle with flour, and fold into thirds. The result should be 6 inches × 2½ feet (15 × 75 cm). Cut across the folds into strips ⅛ inch (½ cm) thick. (If making *soba* noodles, slice into thinner strips.) Gently lift and shake noodles to separate. Sprinkle with flour. Noodles should be elastic, not sticky.

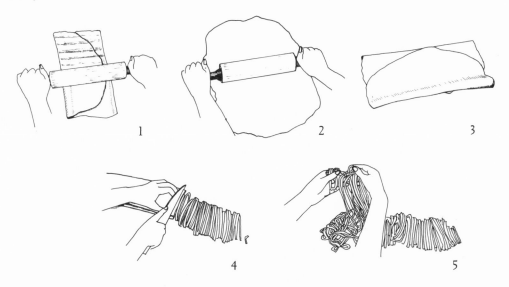

To cook homemade or store-bought noodles

•1. Drop noodles little by little into a large pot containing a generous amount of boiling water. (Use enough water so noodles will separate and boil freely.) Stir to prevent noodles from sticking. Bring to a rolling boil. In a wide circular motion pour 1 cup cold water over noodles. Bring again to a rolling boil. Repeat 3 or 4 times until noodles are *tender throughout but still firm*. Taste frequently. (If using fresh cooked noodles, just reheat as explained in step 4.)

•2. When noodles are done, turn off heat and cover pan for 8 to 10 minutes. (If cooking *soba* noodles, go on to step 3.)

•3. Rinse homemade *udon* noodles in cold running water and stir by hand to remove surface starch. (For store-bought *udon* noodles rinse in cold running water until noodles are cool, then rub vigorously by hand to remove surface starch.) Drain. Rinse *soba* noodles in very cold water, if possible, and treat gently. After rinsing noodles to remove excess surface starch, set aside until ready to serve.

•4. *To serve*: To reheat cooled noodles, put noodles in a colander and set colander in a pot of boiling water (use fresh water) for 1 to 3 minutes. Drain.

Noodles should be served *al dente*, that is, tender but slightly firm at the center. Overcooked noodles go limp and break apart easily.

NOTE: Three basic types of store-bought *udon* and *soba* noodles are sold, and each keeps differently. Dried noodles, stocked on the grocery shelf, keep indefinitely. Fresh cooked or uncooked noodles, found in the refrigerated section of markets (if available), will not keep as long. Fresh cooked noodles must be used within 1 or 2 days; uncooked noodles keep as long as 2 weeks. Refrigerate fresh noodles, unopened, until ready to use. See also *soba* noodles (page 31) and *udon* noodles (page 33).

Fresh-from-the-pot *Udon* Noodles
(Kamaage udon)

This is the simplest and best way to eat udon *noodles. Freshly cooked noodles are dipped in two complementary sauces. Choose one sauce or serve both.*

SERVES 4–5 | 572 Cal. per serving with both sauces

4–5 servings *udon* noodles

SOY DIPPING SAUCE (SERVES 4)
⅓ cup *mirin*
⅓ cup soy sauce
1 cup secondary bonito stock

SESAME DIPPING SAUCE (SERVES 4)
8 Tbsps white sesame seeds
⅓ cup *mirin*
⅓ cup soy sauce
1 cup secondary bonito sauce
1 tsp sugar

CONDIMENTS
3–4 green onions, finely chopped
1-inch (2½-cm) piece fresh ginger, finely grated
1 sheet *nori* seaweed, toasted

•1. Cook noodles following package directions or instructions in previous recipe.

•2. Prepare sauces.
SOY DIPPING SAUCE: Bring *mirin* to a boil over high heat in saucepan to evaporate alcohol. Reduce heat to medium, then add soy sauce and bonito stock. Bring to a boil again, then remove from heat.
SESAME DIPPING SAUCE: Toast and grind sesame seeds (see page 30). Bring *mirin* to a boil over high heat. Reduce heat to medium, then add soy sauce, bonito stock, and sugar. Return to a boil. Remove from heat, add sesame seed, and mix well.

•3. Prepare CONDIMENTS. If *nori* seaweed has not been pretoasted, toast by lightly passing shiny side over an open flame several times. Cut into fine shreds with scissors or wrap in a dry cloth and crumble into small pieces.

•4. Noodles can be served with one or both sauces. Provide every diner with a bowl of each dipping sauce. Reheat noodles (preceding recipe, step 4). Serve noodles in boiled water and set out hot or chilled sauce. Add condiments to sauce according to taste.

Udon or *Soba* Noodles with Egg and Vegetable
(Tamago toji udon *or* soba)

Egg, vegetables, and nori *seaweed give this dish nutritional balance. Try your own favorite vegetables. Serve noodles in piping hot broth and eat while they are firm and at their best. In order to do just that, the Japanese suck in air as they eat hot noodles in broth. This accounts for the loud slurping sounds that surprise the Western ear.*

4 servings *udon* or *soba* noodles
½ cup secondary bonito stock
2 rounded Tbsps green peas
1 sheet *nori* seaweed, toasted
2 leeks
4 eggs

BROTH
4 cups secondary bonito stock
½ cup soy sauce
½ cup *mirin*

•1. Cook noodles following package directions or instructions on page 109.

•2. Prepare 4½ cups bonito stock (see page 36).

•3. Cook peas. If *nori* seaweed has not been pretoasted, toast by lightly passing shiny side over an open flame several times. Cut into fine shreds with scissors or wrap in a dry cloth and crumble into small pieces.

•4. Combine BROTH ingredients in a saucepan and bring to a boil over medium heat. Slice leeks diagonally into 1-inch (2½-cm) lengths, add to boiling broth, and cook until tender-crisp.

•5. Mix eggs with ½ cup *cool* bonito stock. Beat well, frothing as little as possible. Pour into broth in a fine stream, stirring egg mixture as you add it to broth. *Do not stir broth.* When last egg threads set, remove immediately from heat.

•6. Reheat noodles for serving (page 109, step 4). Divide cooked noodles among 4 large, deep soup bowls. Add broth mixture. Sprinkle on green peas and *nori* seaweed. Serve.

Udon Noodles in a Pot
(Nabeyaki udon)

A favorite on a cold day, this dish is chock full of tasty ingredients. Cook in individual flameproof (not ovenproof) casseroles and serve each portion piping hot in its own casserole. Naturally, a deep electric skillet or a large casserole can also be used. Hearty winter fare.

4 servings *udon* noodles
4 dried *shiitake* mushrooms (optional)
2 tsps soy sauce
1 Tbsp sugar
4 leaves fresh spinach with stems
2 leeks
4 oz (115 g) or 4 slices chicken breast
saké
4 eggs
seven-spice mixture (*shichimi*) or ground red pepper (optional)

BROTH
5½ cups secondary bonito stock
5–6 Tbsps soy sauce
2–3 Tbsps *mirin*

To prepare

•1. If using *shiitake* mushrooms, soak in 2 cups warm water until soft (about 1 hour), keeping them submerged by covering with drop-lid (see page 91), flat pan lid, or saucer. Reserve liquid. Discard stems and notch a decorative cross design on caps (see page 63). Add caps, 1 to 1 ½ cups soaking water from mushrooms, soy sauce, and sugar to a saucepan and cook uncovered over a medium heat until tender (15–20 minutes).

•2. Cook noodles following package directions or instructions on page 109.

•3. In a saucepan combine BROTH ingredients. Bring to a boil over medium heat. Reduce heat; let simmer.

•4. Blanch spinach in boiling water. Drain. Cut into 2-inch (5-cm) lengths. Cut leeks diagonally into 1-inch (2 ½-cm) pieces. Lightly season chicken slices with salt and saké.

To assemble

•1. Use 4 individual flameproof (not ovenproof) casseroles with covers (or a single large casserole or a deep electric skillet). Divide cooked noodles into 4 portions. Add spinach, leeks, chicken pieces, and mushrooms. Pour in boiling broth, cover, and bring each casserole to a boil over medium heat.

•2. Make a shallow nest in the center of each portion of noodles and break an egg into each nest. Turn off heat, cover, and serve or allow casseroles to sit 1 or 2 minutes until egg is partially cooked. (If using a large casserole or electric skillet, divide ingredients among 4 large *preheated* soup bowls, add egg, and serve.)

•3. Serve in individual casseroles (or bowls). Season with seven-spice mixture or red pepper to taste.

VARIATION: Shrimp tempura goes well with this dish. Deep-fry 4 large shrimp (see page 138) and place atop noodles just before serving.

Soba Noodles in a Basket
(Zaru soba)

Traditionally served on a flat woven basket sieve (zaru) or a boxlike slatted tray (both of which allow noodles to drain completely), this dish is an ideal hot-weather food for flagging appetites. Hachiwari ("Eighty-percent") soba noodles, so named because it is eighty percent buckwheat flour, are the best and worth searching for. To make homemade soba noodles use 4 cups buckwheat flour to 1 cup all-purpose flour and follow directions for Homemade Udon or Soba Noodles (page 108).

SERVES 4 281 Cal. per serving

10 oz (285 g) dried *soba* noodles

SOY DIPPING SAUCE
⅓ cup *mirin*
⅓ cup soy sauce
1 cup secondary bonito stock

CONDIMENTS
1 sheet *nori* seaweed, toasted
2 tsps *wasabi* horseradish
3–4 green onions, thinly sliced
    seven-spice mixture (*shichimi*) or ground red pepper (optional)

•1. Cook noodles according to package directions or follow instructions on page 109. After cooling and rinsing noodles (page 109, step 3), set aside and allow to drain *well*.

•2. Prepare SOY DIPPING SAUCE (see page 110). Force-cool by swirling bowl with dipping sauce in a larger bowl containing water and ice cubes.

•3. Prepare CONDIMENTS. If *nori* seaweed has not been pretoasted, toast by lightly passing shiny side over an open flame several times. Cut into fine shreds with scissors or wrap in a dry cloth and crumble into small pieces.

•4. Place well-drained noodles on a plate. Sprinkle with *nori* seaweed. Serve with a bowl of dipping sauce. Mix *wasabi* horseradish and green onions into sauce. Season with seven-spice mixture or red pepper, if desired.

Chilled *Somen* Noodles
(Hiyashi somen)

Like Udon Noodles in a Basket, *this is a good dish for sultry summer evenings. Somen noodles—often served with only dipping sauce and condiments—can be livened up with additions such as shrimp or mushrooms. Float noodles in a glass bowl with ice cubes for an enchanting effect. A light refreshing meal.*

SERVES 4	647 Cal. per serving with optional items

10–14 oz (285–400 g) *somen* noodles

DIPPING SAUCE
1½ cups soaking water from mushrooms or secondary bonito stock
6-inch (15-cm) piece kelp (*konbu*)
1 cup loose bonito flakes (*hana-katsuo*), about ⅔ oz (20 g)
⅓ cup soy sauce
⅓ cup *mirin*
1 tsp sugar

CONDIMENTS
3–4 green onions, finely chopped
1 sheet *nori* seaweed, toasted
wasabi horseradish or 1½ inches (4 cm) fresh ginger, finely grated

OPTIONAL ITEMS

4 dried *shiitake* mushrooms
1½ cups soaking water from mushrooms
1½ Tbsps sugar
1½ Tbsps soy sauce
1 Tbsp *mirin*

4 oz (115 g) boned chicken breast without skin
3 Tbsps saké
¼ tsp salt

8 shrimp with shells intact
1 Tbsp saké
½ tsp salt

1 cup egg "tofu" (see page 76)

To prepare

•1. Soak mushrooms in 3½ cups warm water until soft (about 1 hour), keeping them submerged by covering with drop-lid (see page 91), flat pan lid, or saucer. Reserve liquid.

•**2.** Sprinkle chicken fillet with saké and salt. Preheat skillet over medium heat, add chicken, reduce to low heat, and cover. Cook until liquid is absorbed and chicken is no longer pink when pierced (about 7–8 minutes). Add a little more saké if liquid is absorbed before chicken is done. Cool. Shred chicken meat by hand.

•**3.** Devein shrimp (see page 38) by inserting a toothpick at second joint, but do not remove shells. Bring ½ cup water to a boil. Add shrimp, saké, and salt. Cook over medium heat until shrimp turns pink (about 1 minute). Drain. After shrimp has cooled, remove shells.

•**4.** Drain mushrooms, discard stem, and notch a decorative cross design on caps (see page 63). Combine mushrooms with 1½ cups water reserved from soaking (or secondary bonito stock), sugar, soy sauce, and *mirin*. Cook over medium heat until liquid is absorbed.

•**5.** DIPPING SAUCE: Combine dipping sauce ingredients in a clean saucepan. Lightly wipe both sides of kelp with a damp cloth and make ½-inch (1½-cm) cuts with scissors at 1-inch (2½-cm) intervals (see page 35). Bring sauce to a boil over medium heat and remove kelp just *before* water boils. Reduce heat to low and simmer, uncovered, for 5 minutes. Pour through cheesecloth-lined strainer. Force-cool by swirling bowl with dipping sauce in a larger bowl containing water and ice cubes.

•**6.** Prepare CONDIMENTS. If *nori* seaweed has not been pretoasted, toast by passing the shiny side over an open flame several times. Cut into fine shreds with scissors or wrap in a dry cloth and crumble by hand.

To cook noodles

•**1.** Bring ample amount of water to a rapid boil. Add noodles little by little. When water boils again, add ½ cup cold water. Taste a piece of noodle, and if it is tender, remove pot from heat. If noodles are still hard, then bring water to a boil again, add ½ cup cold water, and taste. Repeat this process until noodles are tender.

•**2.** Drain noodles in a colander and transfer to a large bowl. Fill bowl with cold water and rinse well under cold running water for a few minutes. Do not handle noodles while they are still warm. When noodles are completely cooled, rub noodles together by hand for 1 minute to remove surface starch. Drain.

To assemble and serve

•**1.** Because this cold dish is made to refresh on a hot summer day, it is most attractively served on a glass platter or in a glass bowl. Top noodles with shrimp, mushrooms, chicken, and egg tofu. *Somen* noodles may also be served chilled in ice water; optional items are then presented on a serving platter.

•**2.** Serve dipping sauce in individual bowls. Mix *wasabi* horseradish (or ginger) into dipping sauce to taste. Add small amount of chopped onion and shredded *nori* to dipping sauce. Dip noodles into sauce. Replenish condiments as desired.

Cucumber Pickles
(Kyuri no shoyu-zuke)

In Japan, a Japanese-style meal is not complete without a side dish of pickled vegetables. This cucumber dish, which resembles a Western-style salad more than it does Western-style pickles, takes only a few minutes to prepare. Cutting the cucumber into asymmetrical wedges allows the seasonings to penetrate better and thus heightens the flavor. It can be served as soon as 20 minutes after it is prepared, but is best after refrigerated for 24 hours. Try carrots cut into julienne strips, water-cress, or celery.

SERVES 4	20 Cal. per serving

10 oz (285 g) cucumber
1 tsp white sesame seeds
2 Tbsps soy sauce

4–5 rounded Tbsps loose bonito flakes (*hana-katsuo*)

•1. Toast sesame seeds (see page 30). Peel and seed cucumber, then quarter lengthwise. Cut into bite-sized wedges by making a diagonal cut, rotating a quarter turn, and cutting again. Wrap in a dry cloth to remove excess surface moisture.

•2. Combine cucumber, soy sauce, sesame seeds, and bonito flakes in a glass, enamel, or plastic bowl. Do not use a metal bowl. Mix well.

•3. Cover and refrigerate for 20 minutes before serving. Keeps as long as 4 or 5 days. Serve with main course as a side dish.

Lemony Pickled Turnips
(Kabu no remon-zuke)

SERVES 4–6	21 Cal. per serving

18 oz (500 g) medium-sized
  turnips with greens

zest from ½ lemon
2 tsps salt

•1. Trim all but ¾ inch (2 cm) of stem from turnips, reserving greens. Peel turnips from bottom to top, leaving ¾-inch (2-cm) length of stem intact. Wash well in cold water, separating stems at base to remove any trapped dirt. (A toothpick works well.) Cut turnips lengthwise into ¼-inch (¾-cm) thick slices.

•2. Use only the tender lower part of greens. Wash and cut into 1½-inch (4-cm) lengths.

•3. Wash lemon half. Remove zest, being careful to avoid the white pith, which is bitter. Cut zest into very fine slivers.

•4. Place cut greens in a glass, enamel, or plastic bowl. Do not use a metal container. Knead stems, crushing them with your fingers to break fibers and release moisture. Add turnip slices, lemon zest, and salt. Mix *gently* by hand to avoid bruising turnip slices.

•5. Place plate on mixture and add weight that is twice as heavy as turnips and greens. Cover bowl with newspaper. Set aside 24 hours (although it is possible to eat pickles within 2 hours after preparation). Store, refrigerated, in an airtight container for up to 3 days.

Quick Pickled Vegetables
(Ichiya-zuke)

A colorful abundance of fresh vegetables are sliced into thin pieces or slivers and "pickled" for several hours. This recipe calls for 1½ pounds (685 grams) of vegetables, but the amount can easily be adjusted. Use 1 teaspoon salt for every ½ pound (225 grams) of vegetables.

SERVES 4	35 Cal. per serving

½ eggplant, about 5 oz (140 g)
1 cucumber, about 8 oz (225 g)
⅓ carrot, about 2 oz (60 g)

1½ inches (4 cm) fresh ginger
3–4 cabbage leaves, about 9 oz (250 g)
1 scant Tbsp salt

•1. Prepare vegetables.
Eggplant: Trim cap and discard. Cut eggplant into quarters lengthwise, slice thinly, and soak in cold water for 10 minutes. Drain. Wrap in cheesecloth and squeeze out excess moisture.
Cucumber: Peel and seed. Cut into quarters lengthwise and slice thinly.
Carrot and ginger: Peel and cut into very thin slivers.
Cabbage: Finely shred.

•2. Firmly knead salt and vegetables together by hand for about 1 minute to release moisture. Pat down mixture in a bowl, cover with plastic wrap, and top with a plate that covers as much surface area as possible. Place a 2-lb (1-kg) weight on top of plate and refrigerate. (A 2-cup measuring cup filled with water works well.) Can be served as soon as 2 or 3 hours later, but is best 4 or 5 hours after preparation. Keeps 2 to 3 days in winter.

SWEETS

Plum Wine Gelatin
(Umeshu-kan)

Plum Wine Gelatin will appeal to those who like a sophisticated dessert. Agar-agar, a clear gelatin made from a type of red seaweed, congeals very quickly and is easy to unmold. The potency of one bar of agar-agar remains basically the same regardless of slight variations in dimensions.

SERVES 6	118 Cal. per serving

2½ tsps agar-agar (*kanten*) powder
   or 1 bar agar-agar, about 10 ×
   1¼ × 1¼ inches (25 × 3 × 3 cm)
⅔ cup sugar
½ cup plum wine (*umeshu*)
1 Tbsp lemon juice

•1. Rinse agar-agar bar. Soak in cold water for at least 30 minutes. If using powdered agar-agar, skip steps 1 and 3.

•2. Squeeze out water and shred into a 1½-quart (1½-liter) saucepan (or add powder). Add 1¾ cups cold water. Bring to a boil over medium heat, stirring occasionally, and continue to boil until agar-agar dissolves (1–2 minutes).

•3. If using agar-agar bar, pass liquid through cheesecloth-lined wire strainer into a small bowl. Squeeze all liquid from cheesecloth into bowl.

•4. Return liquid to *clean* saucepan. Add sugar. Boil gently over medium heat until quantity is reduced by half and color turns slightly yellow. (Quantity can be checked by dipping a wooden spoon into saucepan and noting level.) Skim off foam.

•5. Add plum wine and lemon juice to gelatin and mix thoroughly. Pour into gelatin mold or a small pan. Set aside. Congeals at room temperature, but will become firmer when refrigerated.

•6. To serve, cut into ½-inch (1½-cm) cubes and arrange in champagne glasses or cut into 3-inch (8-cm) squares and serve on small dessert plates.

Strawberries in Bubbles of Snow
(Ichigo no awayuki-kan)

This dessert is simple to make, congeals in 30 minutes, looks impressive, and is light and delicate. Already possessing all the qualities to become a cook's delight, it will no doubt become a family favorite. Try this dessert with peeled and halved kiwi fruit.

SERVES 6–9   71 Cal. per serving

2½ tsps agar-agar (*kanten*) powder
   or 1 bar agar-agar, about 10 ×
   1¼ × 1¼ inches (25 × 3 × 3 cm)
⅔ cup sugar
2 egg whites
1 Tbsp lemon juice
6–8 strawberries, washed and hulled

•1. Follow steps 1 through 4 in Plum Wine Gelatin (see preceding recipe), but use 2 cups water. (If using muffin pan in step 3, line with plastic wrap now.)

•2. Beat egg whites with a wire whisk or electric hand mixer until soft peaks form. Add agar-agar in a fine stream while continuing to beat egg white (a little assistance may be required for this step). *Continue to beat mixture for 1 minute longer.* Mix in lemon juice.

•3. ***Muffin pan:*** Line each cup with a 6-inch (15-cm) square of clear plastic wrap. Spoon in about ¼ cup "snow," push a whole strawberry into center of each, and bring up plastic wrap, twisting ends to form a ball. Do this fairly quickly, because snow soon stiffens.

Cake pan: Use a small, square cake pan. Moisten pan with water. Spoon in snow and arrange whole strawberries, bottom end up, in several rows with bottoms just peeking out for easier cutting later on. Spread snow around with rubber spatula, if necessary.

•4. Congeals, uncovered, in about 30 minutes. Unwrap snow balls to serve. The snow prepared in a pan should be cut to expose strawberries.

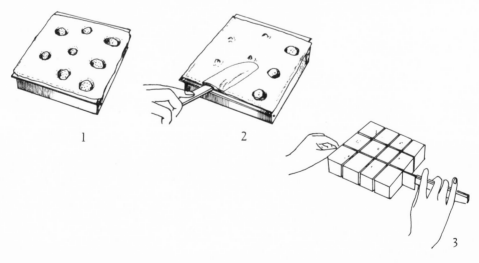

1   2   3

"Wind in the Pines" Miso Cake
(Miso matsukaze)

Unpretentious and tasty, the flavor is subtle and elusive, lending credibility to the name of this cake.

SERVES 6   205 Cal. per serving

2–2½ Tbsps red miso with low to
   medium salt content
1 cup sugar
2 small egg whites
1¼ cups flour
1 tsp baking powder

•1. Blend miso and sugar. Add 1 scant cup water. Stir thoroughly with a wire whisk to remove lumps.

•2. Beat eggs until stiff peaks form. Combine with miso mixture.

•3. Sift together flour and baking powder. Sift again into the egg-and-miso mixture. Mix well. Pour into a small cake pan lined with wax paper. Cover pan with foil and pierce in several places.

•4. Bake in a preheated oven (400°F/205°C) in a large pan of hot water for about 50 minutes or until a toothpick inserted comes out clean.

•5. Cut and serve hot or at room temperature. (If a browned top is desired, add cake—top side down—to lightly oiled and heated skillet and cook over medium heat until browned.)

Sweet Potato Purée with Chestnuts
(Satsuma-imo no chakin shibori)

This traditional sweet potato confection goes well with hot green tea. Top with chestnuts, mold, and serve as a dessert or afternoon snack. Try walnuts in place of chestnuts. Eat with dessert forks or spoons.

SERVES 6   248 Cal. per serving

1 lb (450 g) sweet potatoes
3 Tbsps syrup from canned chestnuts
¾ cup sugar
3 Tbsps *mirin*
salt
8–10 small whole chestnuts pre-
   served in sugar syrup

•**1.** Cut potato into ½-inch (1½-cm) rounds and trim away the slightly discolored outer section, or "ring," just below the skin (about ⅛ inch [½ cm]) and discard. Soak remaining potato in cold water for about 30 minutes.

•**2.** Drain potato and place in a saucepan with enough cold water to barely cover. Bring to a boil. As soon as water boils, replace with cold water. Repeat this step 2 or 3 times until potatoes are soft. Return drained potatoes to saucepan and heat for a few seconds to remove moisture. Shake pan to prevent sticking.

•**3.** Purée sweet potatoes in a food processor (about 2 minutes). Transfer to saucepan and blend in syrup from canned chestnuts, sugar, *mirin*, and salt. Stir vigorously over medium-high heat until smooth. Remove from pan.

•**4.** Holding an 8-inch (20-cm) square of plastic wrap in one hand, mound 1 heaping Tbsp potato purée in center and top with a chestnut, round side up. Bring ends of plastic wrap up and twist to form purée into a ball with chestnut just peeking out of the top. Unwrap and serve on a small dessert plate with dessert fork (or spoon).

Twice-cooked Egg Cake
(Shigure)

A sweet often prepared at New Year, Twice-cooked Egg Cake continues to find favor with each new generation despite the popularity of flour-based Western-style cakes.

SERVES 4–6   135 Cal. per serving

5 eggs
7 Tbsps sugar
1 tsp powdered *matcha* tea (optional)

•**1.** Hard-boil small eggs for 10 minutes (large eggs for 12 minutes). Eggs should be thoroughly hard-boiled.

•**2.** Separate whites and yolks. Press each through fine wire sieve, using the back of a wooden spoon (or mash each with fork).

•**3.** To egg yolk, add 5 Tbsps sugar and pinch salt. Force again through a sieve. To egg white, add 2 Tbsps sugar and pinch salt.

•**4.** Combine powdered tea with egg white. In a 5-×-9-inch (13-×-23-cm) loaf pan, spread green (or white) egg mixture in an even layer. Over first layer spread egg yolk. Cover pan with foil and pierce foil.

•**5.** Place in a large pan of hot water and bake in a preheated oven (400°F/205°C) for 15 minutes.

•**6.** Cool, cut into 1½-inch (4-cm) squares, and serve. Keeps several days.

Do-it-yourself Sushi
(Temaki-zushi)

Literally "Hand-rolled Sushi," Temaki-zushi is simple and fun to make. Attractively arrange ingredients on a large serving platter and let each person create his or her own culinary masterpiece. You may have seen this informal sushi casually passed over the counter from sushi chef to customer. Other possible ingredients include thinly sliced roast beef, smoked salmon, sliced mushrooms, and sliced watercress mixed with bonito flakes and soy sauce, to name just a few. Try your own ideas. This adaptable dish is ideal for parties (see Intimate Sushi Party, page 144).

SERVES 6	603 Cal. per serving

4 horse mackerel (with skin) or 4–8 raw shrimp
5 oz (140 g) fresh or frozen raw tuna fillet of sashimi quality
3 oz (85 g) canned crab meat
4 Tbsps salmon roe
1 avocado

2 eggs
1 Tbsp sugar
2 Tbsps secondary bonito stock
2 tsps *mirin*
2 tsps saké
vegetable oil

1 cucumber
2 rounded Tbsps loose bonito flakes (*hana-katsuo*)
1 Tbsp soy sauce

2 Tbsps fresh grated ginger
14 sheets *nori* seaweed, toasted
10–20 small sprigs chervil or any delicate herb (optional; perilla [*shiso*] leaves are traditional)
soy sauce
2 tsps *wasabi* horseradish

SUSHI RICE
2½ cups uncooked short-grain rice
6-inch (15-cm) piece kelp (*konbu*)
1 Tbsp saké
4½ Tbsps rice vinegar
3 Tbsps sugar
2 tsps salt

To make sushi rice
Making sushi rice is as easy as cooking plain rice. Sushi rice is boiled in kelp-flavored water accented with a dash of saké. Total preparation time (including 1 hour for draining) is approximately 1 hour and 40 minutes.

121

•1. Wash rice as you would plain rice (see page 101). Drain, cover with cheesecloth, and let stand in a colander for 1 hour. (Soak dry rice that has been on the shelf a while for 30 minutes and drain for 30 minutes, if desired.) While rice is draining, prepare sweet vinegar (step 5) and begin preparing other sushi ingredients. (If using rice cooker, see next step.) In a pinch, draining time can be shortened to 30 minutes.

•2. *Pot method*: After rice has been drained, lightly wipe both sides of kelp with a damp cloth and make ½-inch (1½-cm) cuts with scissors at 1-inch (2½-cm) intervals (see page 35). Add kelp to cooking water (1 cup water for every cup rice) in a heavy, tight-lidded pot neither too large nor too small for the amount of rice to be cooked. Bring to a boil, remove kelp, and add rice and saké.

Rice cooker: While rice is draining, soak kelp in cooking water (1 cup water for every cup rice) for 30 minutes and then discard kelp. After rice has drained and kelp has been discarded, add rice and saké, and cook. Skip step 3.

•3. Bring rice to a boil. Turn heat to high for 30 seconds, then cover, reduce heat to very low, and cook for 12 to 13 minutes.

•4. Turn heat to high for 5 seconds (this removes excess moisture), then turn off. *Do not remove lid.* Let rice stand for 10 to 15 minutes.

•5. While rice is cooking, place rice vinegar, sugar, and salt over low heat until sugar and salt dissolve. Cool.

•6. Sprinkle about 2 Tbsps vinegar mixture in the bottom of a large, shallow wooden bowl. (Wood is ideal, but plastic or glass will do. *Do not use metal.*) Turn out hot rice into bowl and sprinkle on remaining vinegar mixture while mixing rice.

To mix rice, gently toss using a wooden spoon (or a rice paddle). Break up any lumps and continue mixing with a sideways cutting movement of the spoon or paddle, spreading out rice evenly. Treat rice gently and do not mash. To cool, fan rice with newspaper or paper fan. When surface rice is cool, turn rice and continue fanning until rice reaches room temperature.

Cover sushi rice with a damp cloth until ready to use.

NOTE: Sushi rice does not keep well and should be eaten the same day it is prepared. Leftovers can be kept slightly longer (though considerable flavor is lost) if tightly sealed in plastic wrap and left *unrefrigerated*. This does *not* apply to fresh fish. Leftover sushi rice cannot be used in stir-fried dishes.

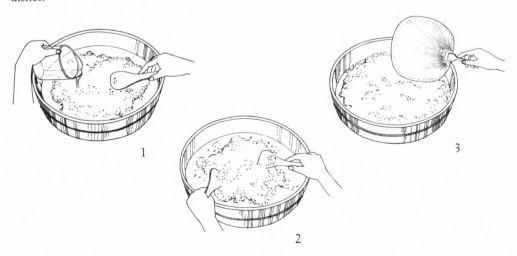

1

2

3

To prepare and serve Do-it-yourself Sushi

•1. Combine egg with sugar, bonito stock, *mirin*, and saké. Beat mixture, frothing as little as possible. Thinly coat a heated skillet with oil and heat again. Add egg mixture and cook over low heat, breaking any bubbles and rotating pan. When bottom is done (but not browned) and egg on top is almost set, flip egg over with spatula and cook other side for a few seconds. Turn out onto a cutting board and allow to cool. Cut lengthwise into ½-inch (1-cm) wide strips. Cut strips into 4-inch (10-cm) lengths.

•2. Prepare remaining ingredients and arrange all of them (except *nori* seaweed) on a large serving platter. Serve cut and toasted *nori* on a separate plate.

Horse mackerel: Gut and fillet. Remove fine bones with tweezers. Slice into slender pieces about ½ inch (1½ cm) wide and 3 inches (8 cm) long.

Shrimp: Prepare as directed in Shrimp Sushi (page 47), but do not soak in rice vinegar.

Tuna: Cut lengthwise into ½-inch (1½-cm) square strips. Cut strips into 4-inch (10-cm) lengths.

Crab: Drain and discard any cartilage.

Salmon roe: Spoon into a small foil bon-bon cup. (Ingredients that contain a lot of liquid should be put in small cups.)

Avocado: Peel and halve. Cut lengthwise into ½-inch (1-cm) wide slices.

Cucumber: Peel and seed. Cut lengthwise into eighths, then into 4-inch (10-cm) lengths. Sprinkle with bonito flakes and soy sauce.

Ginger: Peel, finely grate, and place in a foil bon-bon cup.

Nori Seaweed: If not pretoasted, toast by lightly passing shiny side over an open flame several times to remove moisture and bring out flavor. Cut each sheet into 4 squares. Serve on a separate plate.

•3. Put sushi rice in a large serving bowl accompanied by enough tablespoons to allow everyone to help themselves easily. Distribute individual small dishes or saucers for soy sauce.

•4. *To make sushi*: Place about 1 Tbsp rice on *nori* and gently spread out into oval shape, with more rice towards the upper corner. Add a dab of *wasabi* horseradish and spread with finger or utensil (but use ginger with horse mackerel). Lay chosen ingredients over rice close to the upper corner. Wrap the two flanking corners (corners to left and right) over ingredients so that ingredients protrude from one end while the other end comes to a point. Place one grain of rice on underside of the corner on top and press down to secure. Dip in soy sauce, if desired.

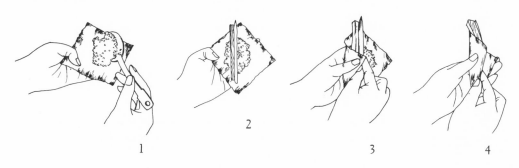

1   2   3   4

Salmon and *Shiitake* Mushroom Sushi

(Sake to shiitake no nigiri-zushi)

Here is a home-style variation of the virtuoso sushi (nigiri-zushi) *served at sushi bars that anyone—even children—can make. Turnip, egg, and lettuce (all optional garnishes) are arranged so that the whole plate suggests a flower in bloom. Make several individual "flowers" or one large platter. In the Japanese tradition of appealing to both the eye and the palate, this lovely sushi dish will bring applause on both counts. Naturally, you can try any of your favorite sushi toppings. Serve with sweet vinegared ginger (see page 27), if desired.*

MAKES APPROX. 24 PIECES	340 Cal. per serving

10–12 oz (285–340 g) smoked salmon

4 large dried *shiitake* mushrooms
1½ Tbsps sugar
2 Tbsps soy sauce

soy sauce
wasabi horseradish

SUSHI RICE
1⅔ cups uncooked short-grain rice
2 Tbsps saké
3 Tbsps rice vinegar
1½ Tbsps sugar
1 tsp salt

OPTIONAL GARNISHES

½ lb (225 g) small turnips, 2–3 turnips
1¼ tsps salt
4 Tbsps rice vinegar
1½ Tbsps sugar
red food coloring (optional)

2 eggs
1 Tbsp sugar
1 tsp rice vinegar
salt

6–8 lettuce leaves (perilla [*shiso*] leaves are traditional)

To prepare

•1. Soak mushrooms in warm water until soft (about 1 hour), keeping them submerged by covering with drop-lid (see page 91), flat pan lid, or saucer. Reserve liquid.

•2. Wash rice and soak in cold water for 30 minutes. Drain for 30 minutes. Prepare SUSHI RICE (see page 121), but do not use kelp.

•3. Peel turnips. Cut crosswise into thin slices. Sprinkle with 1 tsp salt and set aside until soft (about 10 minutes). Rinse and drain. Combine with rice vinegar, sugar, ¼ tsp salt, and red food coloring. Coat well and let stand for 30 to 60 minutes. Drain before using.

•4. Discard stems and combine softened mushrooms with enough liquid from soaking to barely cover mushrooms in a saucepan. Stir in sugar and soy sauce. Simmer over medium heat until liquid is absorbed (about 20 minutes). Slice diagonally into 3 pieces. Cut salmon into 1-×-2-inch (2½-×-5-cm) pieces.

•5. Scramble eggs with sugar, rice vinegar (prevents sticking), and pinch salt over medium heat. Stir constantly until egg is firm but not hard. Fill 4 bon-bon cups with cooked egg.

To assemble and serve

•**1.** Prepare a small amount of dilute vinegar (equal amounts of rice vinegar and water) to moisten hands when shaping sushi rice.

•**2.** Moisten hands with dilute vinegar. Take about 1 rounded Tbsp rice and gently form into a rough oval about 2 inches (5 cm) long. Smooth and finish shaping with fingers of opposite hand. Rotate and shape all sides. Avoid packing so hard that rice is mashed or so loose that it falls apart. Spread a dab of *wasabi* horseradish on underside of each piece of salmon. (Mushrooms are sweet, so do not use *wasabi*.) Place a piece of salmon or mushroom on top and press down with 2 fingers of the opposite hand to secure.

•**3.** Place 1 cup filled with egg in the center of salad plate. Leaving space to lay in lettuce and turnip, arrange 3 pieces mushroom sushi and 3 pieces salmon sushi near rim, radiating out from the center of plate. Tear lettuce to fit, and lean one piece against each piece of sushi. Surround egg with 5 or 6 turnip slices slightly overlapping one another. The result should resemble a flower in full bloom. (For a similar layout using a larger platter, see color plate on page 20.) Serve with soy sauce.

Thin Roll Sushi
(Hosomaki-zushi)

For this and the following two recipes you will need a bamboo rolling mat (see page 130), so check the local oriental outlet. (An undyed or colorfast, flexible place mat or a folded kitchen towel can also be used.) Presented here are the thin sushi rolls—wrapped in nori *seaweed and filled with cucumber, tuna, or gourd ribbons—that often decorate a corner of a sushi platter.* Kappa-maki *is the Japanese name for the popular cucumber-filled roll. Remember, only tuna and cucumber rolls are spiced with* wasabi *horseradish.*

MAKES 8 ROLLS	1070 Cal. total

⅔ oz (20 g) dried gourd ribbons
  (*kampyo*)
1½ Tbsps soy sauce
1½ Tbsps sugar
1½ Tbsps *mirin*

3 oz (85 g) fresh or frozen raw tuna
  fillet of sashimi quality, 7-inch
  (18-cm) long strip, if possible
1 large cucumber
4 sheets *nori* seaweed, toasted
soy sauce
wasabi horseradish
1½ oz (45 g) thinly sliced sweet
  vinegared ginger, about ⅓ cup
  (optional; see page 27)

SUSHI RICE
1¼ cups uncooked short-grain
  rice
2-inch (5-cm) piece kelp (*konbu*)
1 tsp saké
2 Tbsps rice vinegar
2 tsps sugar
1 tsp salt

•1. Prepare SUSHI RICE (see page 121).

•2. *Gourd ribbons*: Cut into 7-inch (18-cm) lengths. Rinse gourd ribbons and scrub with salt. Rinse. Soak in cold water until soft (about 30 minutes). Combine with soy sauce, sugar, *mirin*, and 2 cups water, and simmer with a drop-lid (see page 91) until liquid is absorbed.
Tuna: Cut into strips ¾ × ¾ × 7 inches (2 × 2 × 18 cm).
Cucumber: Peel and seed, then cut into strips about ¾ × ¾ × 7 inches (2 × 2 × 7 cm).

•3. Prepare a small bowl of dilute vinegar (equal amounts of rice vinegar and water) to moisten hands when spreading sushi rice. If *nori* seaweed has not been pretoasted, toast by lightly passing shiny side over an open flame several times.

•4. Cut *nori* in half crosswise. Lay flat side of bamboo mat face up and place shiny side of *nori* face down on mat with longest side facing you. Moisten hands with dilute vinegar. Spread rice. (To spread rice and roll up sushi, see page 128.) Add a dab of *wasabi* horseradish and spread across the middle of the rice with your finger. Top with a strip of cucumber. Roll up. Repeat, making 2 more rolls of cucumber, 3 rolls of tuna, and 2 rolls of gourd ribbon. Do not use *wasabi* with gourd ribbon.

•5. Dip cloth into dilute vinegar and dampen both sides of a sharp knife. Cut each roll into 4 equal pieces. Start with the rolls made first in order to allow the rolls made last to sit 1 or 2 minutes. Clean and remoisten knife as often as necessary. Stand sushi on end (hide messy end), place on a flat plate, and serve with some sweet vinegared ginger slices. Dip in soy sauce, if desired.

Thick Roll Sushi
(Futomaki-zushi)

Thick Roll Sushi, which is being offered with increasing regularity in Japanese restaurants outside Japan, packs six ingredients into a nori-wrapped roll. The rolling technique is easily mastered with a little practice. Use the combined ingredient list when gathering ingredients and checking supplies, but refer to the chart for an easy-to-follow breakdown by major ingredients.

MAKES 4 ROLLS	674 Cal. per roll
3–4 dried *shiitake* mushrooms	1 ½ oz (45 g) thinly sliced sweet vinegared ginger, about ⅓ cup (optional; see page 27)
½ oz (15 g) dried gourd ribbons (*kampyo*)	
6 oz (170 g) canned tuna	7 Tbsps sugar
2 eggs	3 ½ Tbsps soy sauce
9-inch (23-cm) carrot	3 Tbsps secondary bonito stock
4 spinach leaves with stems	2 Tbsps saké
4 sheets *nori* seaweed, toasted	1 Tbsp *mirin*
8 Tbsps chopped red vinegared ginger (optional; see page 27)	soy sauce

SUSHI RICE

2½ cups uncooked short-grain
  rice
6-inch (15-cm) piece kelp (*konbu*)
2 Tbsps saké
4½ Tbsps rice vinegar
3 Tbsps sugar
1 Tbsp salt

<u>Mushrooms</u>
3–4 dried *shiitake* mushrooms
1½ Tbsps sugar
1½ Tbsps soy sauce
1 Tbsp *mirin*
2 cups soaking water from mushrooms

<u>Gourd ribbons</u>
½ oz (15 g) dried gourd ribbons (*kampyo*)
2 Tbsps sugar
2 Tbsps soy sauce
2 cups water

<u>Tuna</u>
6 oz (170 g) canned tuna
2 Tbsps saké
1½ Tbsps sugar
¼ tsp salt

<u>Egg</u>
2 eggs
3 Tbsps secondary bonito stock
¼ tsp salt
1½ Tbsps sugar

<u>Carrot</u>
9-inch (23-cm) carrot
2 tsps sugar
1¼ cups water
pinch salt

<u>Spinach</u>
4 spinach leaves with stems
pinch sugar

To prepare

•1. Prepare SUSHI RICE (see page 121).

•2. For specific amounts used in preparing all items (except *nori* seaweed) in this step, refer to chart.

Mushrooms: Wash. Soak in 2½ cups warm water until soft (about 1 hour), keeping them submerged by covering with drop-lid (see page 91), flat pan lid, or saucer. Reserve liquid. Discard stems. Combine caps in a saucepan with sugar, soy sauce, *mirin*, and reserved soaking liquid plus enough water to make 2 cups liquid. Cook until liquid is nearly absorbed. Cut into ½-inch (1-cm) wide strips.

Gourd ribbons: Cut into 9-inch (23-cm) lengths. Rinse gourd ribbons and scrub with salt. Rinse. Soak in cold water until soft (about 30 minutes). Combine with sugar, soy sauce, and water. Cook with drop-lid over medium heat until liquid is absorbed.

Tuna: Drain well. Flake with a fork, then wrap in cheesecloth, bring ends up, and twist to squeeze out as much liquid as possible. Turn out into a saucepan and add saké, sugar, and salt. Cook over medium-high heat, stirring constantly, until tuna is dry and flaky.

Egg: Combine egg with bonito stock, salt, and sugar. Beat, frothing as little as possible. Cook egg as in Do-it-yourself Sushi (see page 123). Cut into ½-inch (1-cm) wide strips.

Carrot: Peel and cut lengthwise into eighths. Combine with salt, sugar, and water in a saucepan and cook over high heat until liquid is absorbed.

Spinach: Cook as in Dressed Spinach (see page 97). Trim stem ends but do not cut.

Nori *seaweed*: If *nori* has not been pretoasted, toast by lightly passing shiny side over an open flame several times.

To assemble

•**1.** Prepare a small bowl of dilute vinegar (equal amounts of rice vinegar and water) to use to moisten hands while spreading sushi rice.

•**2.** Lay flat side of bamboo rolling mat (see page 130) face up. Place shiny side of *nori* face down on mat with longer side of *nori* facing you. Line up edge of *nori* with edge of mat closest to you.

•**3.** With hands moistened with dilute vinegar, spread about one-quarter of sushi rice on *nori*. Do not pack down rice. Place rice in the center of the *nori* sheet and carefully spread it out toward the edges with the fingertips, making a layer about ½ inch (1 cm) thick. Remoisten hands as often as necessary. Leave upper 1 inch (2½ cm) of *nori* farthest from you free of rice.

•**4.** Divide egg and tuna each into 4 equal portions. Place fillings down the center, extending from one side to the other about one-third the way up from the edge closest to you: Lay 4 or 5 gourd ribbons down first and top with tuna. Make a row of sliced mushrooms alongside tuna, top with egg, 2 strips of carrot, and 1 piece spinach. For added color, add 2 Tbsps red vinegared ginger.

•**5.** To roll, hold the fillings in place with your fingertips (until you can no longer do so), while rolling the edge of mat and *nori* (closest to you) over fillings. Reposition hands and tuck edge under so that it meets the edge of *rice* (not seaweed). Roll forward slightly, and with the mat still wrapped around it, use gentle pressure to even the roll. (It may take a little practice before you are able to get the ingredients in the center.) Unwrap bamboo mat and complete remaining rolls in the same manner.

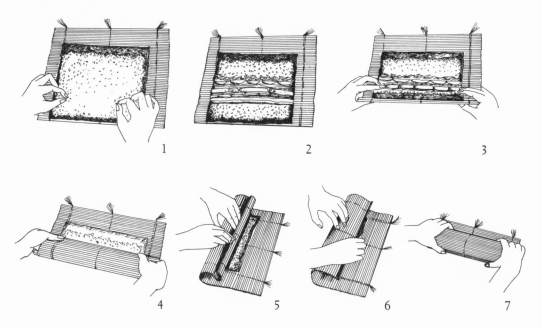

1   2   3

4   5   6   7

•6. Dip cloth into dilute vinegar and dampen both sides of a sharp knife. Cut rolls crosswise into 1-inch (2½-cm) thick sections. (Let roll made last sit 1 or 2 minutes before cutting.) Clean and remoisten knife as often as necessary. Arrange sushi cut side up. Serve with sweet vinegared ginger slices. Dip in soy sauce, if desired.

Cherry Blossom Sushi Roll
(Hana-zushi)

The same rolling technique used in Thick Roll Sushi is utilized here with remarkable results. Don't be afraid to attempt this delightful sushi, because it's easier than it looks. Brace yourself for a flood of compliments.

MAKES 2 ROLLS	590 Cal. per roll

4 dried *shiitake* mushrooms
1½ Tbsps sugar
1½ Tbsps soy sauce
1 Tbsp *mirin*
4 9-inch (23-cm) spinach leaves
   with or without stems
pinch sugar
2 Tbsps finely chopped red
   vinegared ginger (see page 27)
5 sheets *nori* seaweed, toasted
soy sauce

SUSHI RICE
1⅔ cups uncooked short-grain
   rice
2 Tbsps saké
3-inch (8-cm) piece kelp (*konbu*)
3 Tbsps rice vinegar
1½–2 Tbsps sugar
1 tsp salt

To prepare

•1. Prepare SUSHI RICE (see page 121).

•2. Wash mushrooms. Soak in 2½ cups warm water until soft (about 1 hour), keeping them submerged by covering with drop-lid (see page 91), flat pan lid, or saucer. Reserve liquid. Discard stems. Combine caps in a saucepan with the sugar, soy sauce, *mirin*, and liquid from soaking mushrooms plus enough water to make 2 cups. Simmer with a drop-lid until liquid is absorbed. Cut in half.

•3. Cook spinach as in Dressed Spinach (see page 97). Trim stem end but do not cut.

•4. Mix 1½ cups loosely packed sushi rice with chopped red ginger. Divide into 6 equal portions. If *nori* seaweed has not been pretoasted, toast 2 sheets by lightly passing shiny side over an open flame several times. Cut each sheet lengthwise into thirds. Lay flat side of bamboo mat (see following page) face up and place shiny side of *nori* face down on mat with longest side facing you. Spread 1 portion (about 1 rounded Tbsp) pink rice on *nori* and roll (see facing page). Repeat with a second sheet of *nori*. Make six rolls. (These will be the "blossoms.")

To assemble

•1. Toast remaining 3 sheets of *nori*. Place a full sheet, shiny side down, on bamboo mat (flat side up) with longest side of *nori* facing you. Cut 1 sheet in half lengthwise. Join half sheet with whole sheet on mat by placing a few grains of cooked rice at the edge of one (match longer edges), laying the edge of the other sheet so that it covers rice, and pressing down gently with fingers. (Make sure you match sides: shiny side with shiny side; dull with dull.) This "glues" the sheets together. (The glued edges should be parallel to the bamboo slats.)

•2. Prepare a small bowl of dilute vinegar (equal amounts of rice vinegar and water) to use to moisten hands while spreading sushi rice. Moisten hands with dilute vinegar. Spread on sushi rice about ½ inch (1 cm) thick, leaving a 1-inch (2½-cm) space between the upper edge of *nori* and upper edge of rice. (To spread rice and roll up sushi, see page 128.) Using your fingers, make a narrow trough at a distance one-third the way from the edge closest to you. Stand up a row of mushroom halves cut side down. Lay a length of spinach on each side of the mushrooms (trim spinach stems, if necessary). Spread on a little more rice to barely cover spinach and to support pink rice rolls. Stack 3 pink sushi rolls in a pyramid and set them on top of mushrooms and spinach. Hold them securely with one hand and with the other fold the edge of *nori* (closest to you) over all. Roll up. Make a second roll with remaining ingredients. Let rolls stand 1 or 2 minutes.

•3. Dip cloth into dilute vinegar and dampen a sharp knife. Cut rolls crosswise into 1-inch (2½-cm) slices. Clean and remoisten knife as often as necessary. Serve cut side up. Dip in soy sauce, if desired.

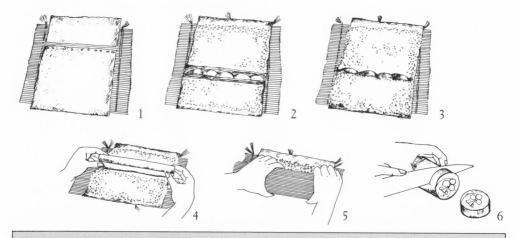

BAMBOO ROLLING MAT (*MAKI-SU*): The rolling mat appears in several recipes, most notably the three rolled sushis (pages 125–30). It is fashioned from thin strips of bamboo held together by durable cotton string that runs the length of the mat every few inches. The rolling technique (page 128) utilizes a bamboo mat to press and shape materials into long cylindrical or squared forms.

This inexpensive utensil is stocked in many Japanese provision outlets. The decorative bamboo or stick place mats offered at low-cost import emporiums may be employed as long as they are undyed (or colorfast) and have not been chemically treated. If bamboo mats or stick place mats are unavailable, improvise with a flexible colorfast place mat or a folded kitchen towel.

Wash mat well using mild soap and store in a dry place after it is thoroughly dry.

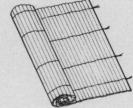

Sushi in a Purse
(Chakin- *or* Fukusa-zushi)

Sushi rice mixed with slivers of simmered vegetables is carefully wrapped in a delicate crepelike egg sheet, which is then shaped into a "purse" and secured with an edible "purse string" of spinach (or gourd ribbon). A round egg sheet will result in a purse with ruffled edges (as shown in sketch), while a square egg sheet can easily be fashioned into a purse with four petal-like flaps (see contents page). Omit the shrimp, if making the bundle-shaped Fukusa-zushi. *This sushi is served without soy sauce or* wasabi *horseradish.*

MAKES 8 PURSES   212 Cal. per serving

2 dried *shiitake* mushrooms
⅓ oz (10 g) dried gourd ribbons
   (*kampyo*)
2 tsps sugar
2 tsps *mirin*
1 Tbsp soy sauce

4 shrimp, about 2 inches (5 cm) long
2 tsps rice vinegar
2 tsps sugar

1-inch (2½-cm) length carrot
1 tsp sugar
10 snow peas
8 spinach stems without leaves or 8
   6-inch (15-cm) strips dried gourd
   ribbon (*kampyo*) for purse strings
1 Tbsp white sesame seeds, toasted
   and chopped (see page 30)
1½ oz (45 g) thinly sliced sweet
   vinegared ginger, about ⅓ cup
   (optional; see page 27)

8 eggs
1 Tbsp sugar
1 tsp *mirin*
½ tsp salt
1½ tsps cornstarch
vegetable oil

SUSHI RICE
1 cup uncooked short-grain rice
5-inch (13-cm) piece kelp (*konbu*)
1 tsp saké
1½–2 Tbsps rice vinegar
2 tsps sugar
⅔ tsp salt

•1. Prepare SUSHI RICE (see page 121).

•2. *Mushrooms and gourd ribbons*: Wash mushrooms. Soak in 1½ cups warm water until soft (about 1 hour), keeping them submerged by covering with drop-lid (see page 91), flat pan lid, or saucer. Reserve liquid. Rinse gourd ribbons and scrub with salt. Rinse. (If using gourd ribbons for purse strings, prepare along with ⅓ oz [10 g] gourd ribbons in this step.) Combine soaked mushrooms and rinsed gourd ribbons in a saucepan with sugar, *mirin*, soy sauce, and 1 cup liquid from soaking mushrooms. Bring to a boil, then simmer until liquid is absorbed. (Set aside 8 gourd ribbon purse strings.) Chop mushrooms and gourd ribbons. *Shrimp*: Cook shrimp in salted water until shells turn pink. Shell and devein (page 38). Cut in half crosswise. Soak in rice vinegar and sugar for 20 minutes.

Remaining vegetables: Peel carrot and cut into fine slivers. Boil until just tender in ½ cup water, 1 tsp sugar, and pinch salt. Drain. Cut snow peas into fine slivers. Cook in salted water until just tender. Drain. Cook spinach purse strings, making sure stems are soft and pliable.

Egg: Combine eggs with sugar, salt, *mirin*, and cornstarch mixed with 2 tsps water. Beat eggs well and filter through cheesecloth. Heat a lightly oiled skillet or egg pan (choose an unscarred skillet that allows for easy maneuvering of egg) over medium heat. Pour in enough egg (egg should sizzle) to *thinly* coat bottom. Tilt pan to spread egg, then pour excess back into bowl. Cook over medium heat, tapping down any bubbles. Adjust heat and move pan about as necessary to cook egg evenly and prevent browning. When egg is almost dry, loosen edges, lift up with fingers (or slip a spatula under egg), and gently flip over. Cook several seconds and then slide onto a plate and cool. Re-oil skillet, heat, and repeat until all egg mixture is used. Sheets should be thin, crepelike, and cooked (but not browned). Make 8 sheets. After egg sheets cool, trim messy edges. Save trimmings.

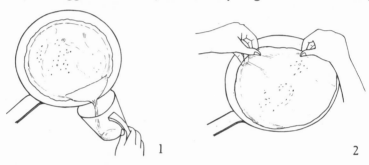

•3. Toss gourd ribbons, mushrooms, snow peas, sesame seeds, carrot, and egg trimmings with sushi rice until well mixed into rice. *Do not mash rice.* Divide into 8 portions. Each portion should be about ⅓ cup loosely packed sushi rice.

•4. Prepare a small bowl of dilute vinegar (equal amounts of rice vinegar and water) to moisten hands.

•5. *Purse* (*Chakin-zushi*): Place egg sheet over the top of a coffee cup. With moistened hands shape 1 portion sushi rice mixture firmly but lightly into 1½-inch (4-cm) ball. Place in center of egg sheet. Lift out egg sheet and bring egg up and around rice. Play with floppy edges to shape purse. Loosely tie with spinach (or gourd ribbon) purse string, leaving a 1-inch (2½-cm) opening. Place shrimp in opening. Garnish with sweet vinegared ginger.

Bundle (*Fukusa-zushi*): Sushi can also be rolled up blintz style. Place rice on lower third of the egg sheet, fold lower edge over rice, fold in sides, and roll up. Shape while folding in edges and rolling to form a rectangular bundle. Secure bundle with spinach (or gourd ribbon) to form a neat little "package." Garnish with sweet vinegared ginger.

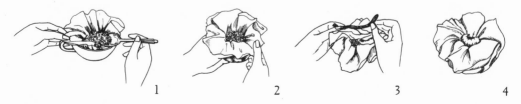

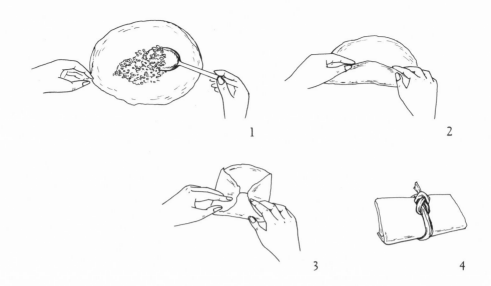

1   2

3   4

Mixed Sushi Bowl
(Gomoku-zushi)

Easily assembled, this "bowl of sushi" is ideal for enjoying a subtle blend of tastes. By simply reserving and sprinkling a bit of each ingredient on top, this home-style dish becomes festive enough for entertaining. Prepare all or some of the ingredients. When gathering ingredients and checking supplies, use the combined ingredient list, but refer to the chart for an easy-to-follow breakdown by major ingredients. Mix well before eating.

SERVES 4   806 Cal. per serving

4 dried *shiitake* mushrooms
¾ oz (22 g) dried gourd ribbons (*kampyo*)
½ lb (225 g) horse mackerel with skin or any sashimi-quality fish fillet
2 oz (60 g) canned lotus root, about 2 inches (5 cm) (optional)
3 eggs
vegetable oil for frying egg
4 oz (115 g) canned bamboo shoots
3 inches (8 cm) carrot
10 shrimp, about 4 oz (115 g)
6 oz (170 g) canned tuna
20 snow peas
1–2 sheets *nori* seaweed, toasted
3 Tbsps finely slivered red vinegared ginger (see page 27)

sesame seeds, toasted (see page 30)
2 cups secondary bonito stock
11 Tbsps (about ⅔ cup) rice vinegar
8½ Tbsps (about ⅗ cup) sugar
4 Tbsps soy sauce
3 Tbsps saké
2½ tsps *mirin*
salt

SUSHI RICE
2½ cups uncooked short-grain rice
6-inch (15-cm) piece kelp (*konbu*)
1 Tbsp saké
4½ Tbsps rice vinegar
3 Tbsps sugar
2 tsps salt

Mushrooms and gourd ribbons
4 dried *shiitake* mushrooms
¾ oz (22 g) dried gourd ribbons (*kampyo*)
2 cups soaking water from mushrooms
2 cups soaking water from gourd ribbons
3 Tbsps sugar
3 Tbsps soy sauce
2 tsps *mirin*

Fish
½ lb (225 g) horse mackerel with skin or
    any sashimi-quality fish fillet
7 Tbsps rice vinegar
salt

Lotus root (optional)
2 oz (60 g) canned lotus root, about 2
    inches (5 cm)
1½ Tbsps sugar
½ tsp salt
3 Tbsps rice vinegar

Egg
3 eggs
½ Tbsp sugar
¼ tsp salt
vegetable oil

Bamboo shoots
4 oz (115 g) canned bamboo shoots
1 cup secondary bonito stock
1 Tbsp sugar
1 Tbsp soy sauce
¼ tsp salt

Carrot
3 inches (8 cm) carrot
1 Tbsp sugar
pinch salt
1 cup secondary bonito stock

Shrimp
10 shrimp, about 4 oz (115 g)
1 Tbsp rice vinegar
1 Tbsp saké
pinch salt

Tuna
6 oz (170 g) canned tuna
2 Tbsps saké
1½ Tbsps sugar
pinch salt

Snow peas
20 snow peas
½ tsp *mirin*
salt

•1. Prepare SUSHI RICE (see page 121).

•2. For specific amounts used in preparing all items (except *nori* seaweed) in this step, see chart.

Mushrooms and gourd ribbons: Wash and soak mushrooms in 2½ cups warm water until soft (about 1 hour), keeping them submerged by covering with drop-lid (see page 91), flat pan lid, or saucer. Reserve liquid. Rinse gourd ribbons and scrub with salt. Rinse. Soak in 2½ cups cold water until soft (about 30 minutes), reserving liquid.

Rinse mushrooms and discard stems. Combine mushrooms and gourd ribbons with 2 cups soaking liquid from mushrooms and 2 cups soaking liquid from gourd ribbons. (Add enough water to make 4 cups, if necessary.) Stir in sugar, soy sauce, and *mirin*. Cook over medium-high heat with drop-lid until liquid is absorbed (about 30 minutes). Thinly slice mushrooms and chop gourd ribbons.

Horse mackerel: Without skinning, sprinkle with salt and set aside for 1 hour. Rinse. (This purifies and firms flesh.) Rinse in 2 Tbsps rice vinegar, add about 5 Tbsps vinegar to barely cover, and set aside for 20 minutes. The skin is then easily removed. Cut fish into thin diagonal strips.

Fish: Cut into thin diagonal strips.

Lotus root (optional): Slice into paper-thin rounds. Reserve 10 whole slices for garnish. Slice remaining lotus into quarters. Place all in glass bowl and add sugar, salt, and vinegar. Drain just before adding to sushi rice.

Egg: Combine egg with sugar and salt. Beat well. Cook egg following directions in Sushi in a Purse (see page 132). After sheets cool, roll up and slice crosswise into fine threads. (Trim messy edges before rolling, if desired.)

Bamboo shoots: Wash thoroughly and remove any white residue. Cut into ½-inch (1½-cm) long julienne strips. Combine bamboo and remaining ingredients. Cover and cook over medium-high heat until liquid is nearly absorbed.

Carrot: Peel and then cut crosswise into paper-thin rounds, stack slices, and cut into slivers. Add carrot, sugar, salt, and enough bonito stock to cover. Cover and cook over medium-high heat until just tender.

Shrimp: Shell and devein (see page 38). Break off tail. Add vinegar, saké, pinch salt, and enough water to cover. Boil shrimp until it turns pink.

Tuna: Drain well. Flake with a fork, then wrap in cheesecloth, bring up ends, and twist to squeeze out as much liquid as possible. Turn out into a saucepan and add saké, sugar, and pinch salt. Stir constantly over medium-high heat until dry and flaky.

Snow peas: Remove stem and strings. Cut lengthwise into fine slivers. Cook in boiling salted water for 1 minute. Drain. Sprinkle with *mirin*.

Nori *seaweed*: If not pretoasted, toast by passing shiny side over an open flame several times. Cut into fine shreds with scissors or wrap in a dry cloth and crumble into small pieces.

•3. *To assemble*: Use a large, shallow serving bowl. Reserve all of shrimp, *nori*, red vinegared ginger, and sesame seeds. In addition, set aside 10 lotus rounds (drained), half of egg, and a small amount of other ingredients. With a wooden spoon, mix remaining ingredients (including egg trimmings) into sushi rice. Sprinkle reserved egg over top, then add other toppings. Finish up with lotus, shrimp, red vinegared ginger, sesame seeds (to taste), and *nori* in that order. (An alternate method calls for about half of egg to be sprinkled over rice, then all of remaining ingredients. Finish up with shrimp, sesame seeds, egg, and *nori*.) Mix well before eating.

YAKITORI

Yakitori

Yakitori's *reputation abroad has been steadily growing in recent years.* Yakitori, *literally "grilled chicken," is a kebab of petit chicken or vegetable morsels grilled over charcoal and basted with a soy sauce-and-mirin mixture or sprinkled with salt. (This salted type is known as shioyaki, literally "salt grilled.") The secret lies in the size of the skewered pieces: they should be 1 inch (2 ½ cm) or less in diameter, a size that allows for perfect grilling. When done, the outside should be barely charred, while the inside should be cooked through but still tender and juicy (and never dry). If the pieces are too large, the outside will burn or become tough by the time the inside is completely cooked.*

Perfect for a barbecue, yakitori can be skewered well in advance, and a supply of sauce can be permanently maintained, ready for use at any time (see following note). For party suggestions, see Yakitori Barbecue Party *(page 143).*

SERVES 4
517 Cal. per serving

1–2 boned chicken breasts with skin
4 oz (115 g) chicken liver
½ clove garlic
3–4 leeks
2 bell peppers
6–10 fresh mushrooms (optional)
salt
seven-spice mixture (*shichimi*) or
   ground red pepper
sansho powder (if available)
20 6-inch (15-cm) bamboo skewers
   (see facing page) or stainless steel
   kebab skewers

YAKITORI SAUCE
½ cup soy sauce
½ cup *mirin*
2½ Tbsps sugar

To prepare

•1. Combine YAKITORI SAUCE ingredients. Cook over medium heat, stirring occasionally, until quantity is reduced by half. Cool. Pour into a wide-mouthed jar (or tall glass) of sufficient depth to allow complete dipping. (If basting, any size container will do.)

•2. Rinse chicken and pat dry. Remove skin. Cut both chicken and skin into bite-sized pieces, about 1 inch (2½ cm) in diameter. Cook skin in boiling water for 5 minutes. Drain.

•3. Rinse liver in salted water. Cut garlic in half. Place liver and garlic in a saucepan with enough water to barely cover. Simmer until surface changes color. Drain.

•4. Cut white portion of leeks into 1-inch (2½-cm) pieces. (Reserve green portion for other uses.) If leek is too thick for easy grilling, cut pieces in half lengthwise, keeping rings together. Seed and cut each bell pepper into 1-inch (2½-cm) squares (or 2-inch [5-cm] long strips). Wash and trim mushrooms.

To assemble and serve

•1. When skewering, do not leave any space between skewered pieces, since bamboo is liable to burn during grilling. Wrap exposed end of each skewer in foil for easy handling.

Skewer chicken and leek alternately (thread leek crosswise) or thread separately, if desired. Thread remaining ingredients as follows: chicken skin, 5 or 6 pieces per skewer; liver, 4 or 5; bell pepper, 3 or 4; mushroom, 3 or 4 (or skewer pepper and mushroom alternately). If livers or mushrooms are too big for easy grilling, cut in half.

•2. Sprinkle salt on half the skewers and keep separate from unsalted skewers. (Unsalted skewers will eventually be dipped in sauce.)

•3. Grill each side of chicken over hot coals until surface of chicken turns white (or until surface of vegetables is almost dry), keeping salted skewers separate from unsalted skewers. Dip *unsalted* skewers in sauce, allow excess to drip back into the jar, grill one side, dip again, and grill other side. Repeat until skewered foods are cooked, turning skewers after each dipping. Turn salted skewers as necessary. Do not overcook. Remember, food should be tender, not dry.

•4. Arrange on serving platter and season with seven-spice mixture (or ground red pepper) or *sansho* powder, if desired.

NOTE: *Yakitori* sauce keeps very well refrigerated in a tightly sealed bottle. Replace the quantity used from time to time. Boil the entire batch at least once a month to ensure freshness and strain after every use. The flavor improves with age.

BAMBOO SKEWERS: Inexpensive and disposable, bamboo skewers are a handy item to have around the kitchen. Foods may be grilled easily (see *Yakitori*, page 136) and appetizers decoratively presented. Wrapping the handle in foil not only serves a decorative purpose but also allows for easier handling while grilling. Points can be strengthened and "tempered" by scorching them until they turn black and then plunging them into cold water. Skewers can be washed and reused several times, if desired. Available at oriental outlets, import emporiums, and many supermarkets.

Thin metal skewers are acceptable substitutes for bamboo skewers, but they should be sharp. Sharpen points on a whetstone. Long metal skewers (10 to 15 inches [25 to 40 cm], depending on the size of the fillet) are required for Quick-seared Bonito Sashimi (page 53).

TEMPURA

Tempura

Producing a good tempura is as simple as making any other deep-fried dish, although it continues to baffle many cooks. Two factors are of major importance: the oil and the batter. Use only fresh vegetable oil (special tempura oil is also available, but not a necessity), and maintain a constant temperature by filling no more than half the surface area at one time and by skimming oil often to remove excess batter. Neglecting either of these simple points will result in a lower oil temperature, and the final outcome will be soggy tempura, a common pitfall that can easily be avoided with a little attention to detail. Make the batter just before deep-frying; that is, after everything else is in readiness (fish, vegetables, oil, utensils). Batter should be lumpy and incompletely mixed, as though it were thrown together by a child, and made in small batches.

One of the beauties of this dish is that you can deep-fry as much (or as little) of each ingredient as you wish. The amounts below are only guidelines. Adjust amounts and substitute ingredients freely. Other acceptable ingredients include scallops, snow peas, asparagus tips, paper-thin slices of fresh ginger, onions (cut in half lengthwise, secure rings with toothpick, and cut crosswise into 3/8-inch [1-cm] thick slices), or any similar food that is fresh or tender.

Tempura should be served immediately, *so try to arrange your meal plan accordingly. See also Tempura on Rice (page 103) and Tempura Party (page 148).*

SERVES 4 · 770 Cal. per serving

8 medium shrimp
6 oz (170 g) any white-fleshed fish
1 squid, about 6 oz (170 g)
3 bell peppers
1 small sweet potato
20 green beans
1/2 sheet *nori* seaweed
3 inches (8 cm) carrot
1 eggplant, about 10 oz (285 g)
4 fresh *shiitake* mushrooms or 4 fresh
   white mushrooms

5–6 cups vegetable (or tempura) oil
   for deep-frying

DIPPING SAUCE
2 cups secondary bonito stock
1/2 cup soy sauce
1/2 cup *mirin*

BATTER
2 large eggs
1 cup ice water
2 cups sifted flour

CONDIMENTS
1 cup finely grated daikon radish or
  white radish
3 inches (8 cm) fresh ginger, finely
  grated

To prepare

•1. Prepare seafood first.

Shrimp: Shell and devein (see page 38), but leave tail and shell segment closest to tail intact. Diagonally cut off a portion of tail and force out moisture with edge of knife. Make 4 or 5 deep crosswise cuts in belly and gently straighten shrimp by pressing down with the thumbs of both hands on rounded topside of shrimp.

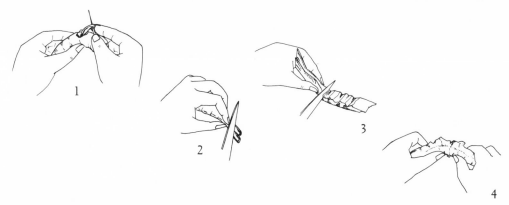

Fish: Fillet and cut into bite-sized pieces. Remove any fine bones with a tweezers.
Squid: Clean (see page 50) and cut into 1- × -3-inch (2½ - × -8-cm) strips. Pat dry. Coat with flour.

•2. Prepare vegetables.

Bell pepper: Seed and cut into 2- to 3-inch (5- to 8-cm) strips about 1 inch (2½ cm) wide. Pierce outer surface of each piece 5 or 6 times with a toothpick.
Sweet potato: Wash and scrape, then cut into ½ -inch (1-cm) thick rounds.
Green beans (and nori *seaweed)*: Cut a strip of *nori* ½ × 2½ inches (1½ × 6½ cm) from sheet. Wrap *nori* strip around middle of a bundle of 4 or 5 green beans. Moisten strip with water and secure. Repeat with remaining green beans. Cut remaining *nori* into 4 equal pieces (for deep-frying).
Carrot: Cut into julienne strips.
Eggplant: Trim stem but leave cap. Quarter lengthwise. Place cut side down, and starting 1 inch (2½ cm) below cap, make 3 or more lengthwise cuts and fan out slices.

Mushrooms: Wash thoroughly and trim stem. (If using fresh *shiitake* mushrooms, discard stems.)

•3. Combine DIPPING SAUCE ingredients and bring to a boil over medium heat. Cool to room temperature.

To deep-fry

•1. Heat vegetable oil in a heavy skillet to medium deep-frying temperature (about 340°F/170°C). Oil depth should be at least twice the thickness of the thickest food to be fried. Test oil temperature by dropping in a bit of batter into oil. If the batter sinks to the bottom and then rises, the oil is not hot enough; if it does not sink, the oil is too hot. When it sinks halfway and then quickly rises to the top, the oil is perfect.

•2. Prepare a wire rack or a plate lined with absorbent paper. Arrange ingredients on a large platter and place close at hand to allow easy dipping and frying.

•3. After all ingredients are arranged and ready for deep-frying and when oil is nearly ready, prepare BATTER. Do not let batter stand. Mix egg and water first, then add flour all at once and *mix slightly* with fork or chopsticks. Batter ingredients should be loosely combined so that batter is lumpy. Clumps of flour should still be floating on surface. If overmixed, batter will be heavy and sticky when deep-fried. If cooking larger amounts of tempura, make batter in batches rather than making a large amount at one time.

•4. Dip each item in batter, shake off excess, and fry until food is cooked and batter creamy or beige (see step 5). Several ingredients require special cooking instructions.

Shrimp: Dip into batter up to tail. Slip gently into oil holding tail for several seconds, then releasing. When shrimp comes to the surface, turn and cook other side.

Carrot: Take 5 or 6 strips carrot between thumb, middle and index fingers. Dip bottom third of carrot bundle into batter, scooping up a generous amount of batter. Dip into oil, batter end first, and allow batter end to cook for 15 seconds before releasing bundle.

Nori *Seaweed*: Dip dull side in batter. Slip, batter side down, into oil and turn in about 1 minute (or less). Remove. Drain batter side down.

•5. Seafood requires a slightly higher temperature (360°F/180°C) than vegetables (340°F/170°C), while *nori* and light vegetables (such as snow peas) are fried at a lower temperature (320°F/160°C). In general, cook heavier foods first and fragile foods last.

Do not fill more than half the surface area of oil when frying. Crowding causes oil temperature to fall, and the result will be soggy tempura.

Skim off excess pieces of floating batter often. An accumulation of batter also reduces the temperature.

Important: Tempura is done when coating is creamy or beige (or sometimes a pale yellow). The final color is *light*. It should not be cooked until "golden brown" as is done with fried chicken. Foods should be cooked through but still retain their texture. Carrots and green beans should be tender-crisp, sweet potatoes firm but cooked, and so on.

To serve

•1. Serve tempura immediately. Line serving dish or individual plates with absorbent paper. Arrange tempura decoratively.

•2. Serve dipping sauce at room temperature in individual dipping bowls (⅓ to ½ cup sauce in each). Set out grated daikon and grated ginger. Each is added to dipping sauce according to taste (about 1 Tbsp daikon and ½ tsp ginger). Replenish sauce and condiments as desired.

VARIATION: A mixed-ingredient tempura is a tasty alternative. Coarsely chopped shrimp and leek is only one of numerous possibilities. Experiment and create your own.

Mix chopped ingredients of your choice. Coat ⅓ cup of chosen ingredients with tempura batter. Gently slide mixture into oil against side of pan. Do not drop into the center, or ingredients will spread out too much. You have a few seconds to shape patty before batter sets. Break patty surface to allow oil to penetrate and wait several seconds, then pat lightly with utensil to smooth surface. Turn when done and cook other side, again breaking surface in several places. Oil temperature should be medium (340°F/170°C). Remove and drain. Finished tempura patty will be approximately 4 inches (10 cm) in diameter.

GRATER: In Japanese cooking, the grater plays a simple but important role by making fresh ingredients readily accessible for daily use. While the typical household grater will suffice, the Japanese two-in-one graters that have surfaces for grating both daikon radish (fine) and ginger (very fine) and that catch the grated material (and any resultant liqid) either in a box below or in a depression at the farthest end are worth searching for because they are easy to use and clean, and make what has always been a somewhat messy operation a very simple procedure, eliminating the need for additional bowls and cheesecloths.

Perhaps the easiest to use, especially when grating large quantities, is the box-shaped grater: spikes surround holes, gratings are caught in the box below, and the top (the grating surface) slides out for easy access to grated material. The tray-shaped grater, which has spikes but no holes and catches gratings and liquid at the farthest end, is useful for grating small amounts without fuss.

If using a multipurpose Western grater, grate daikon, (or white radish or turnip) over a bowl. Use a fine surface to grate daikon but not so fine as to turn it into a liquid pulp. Drain off most, but not all, of the water (but do not squeeze). You should be able to mound grated daikon to a certain extent. If not, use a coarser grating surface.

Use the finest surface to finely grate ginger or to make ginger juice. Grate onto a cheesecloth placed over a small bowl. Squeeze the cheesecloth to extract juice. Juice may also be obtained by grating ginger and squeezing grated material with your fingers.

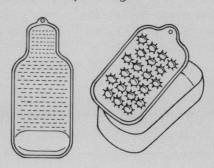

Cocktail Party Menu

• Smoked Salmon and Daikon Rolls (page 42) • Skewered Chicken Quenelles (page 43) • Chicken-stuffed Squash Balls (page 44) • Soft Simmered Chicken Gizzards (page 44) • Pork and Vegetable Kebabs (page 46) • Shrimp Sushi (page 47)

A tour de force of Japanese appetizers, this menu showcases an array of exotic and innovative treats and is the perfect touch for an enjoyable afternoon or evening of drinks and socializing.

Party tips

Cocktail parties can be one of the most enjoyable and relaxing forms of entertaining for both host and guest. It is a chance for the enterprising cook to experiment, create, and receive numerous evaluations of his or her skills, and a chance for the guests to try a variety of tasty foods under a canopy of informality.

One key to a successful cocktail party is variety. The above menu can be expanded almost effortlessly by including Sashimi Platter Supreme (page 51). Since the menu is only a guideline, add or substitute recipes freely. Other possibilities are Salmon and *Shiitake* Mushroom Sushi (page 124), Deep-fried Chicken Nuggets (page 59), and any of the rolled sushis (pages 125–30).

There is always a great temptation to double or triple recipes to meet the expected demand. In general, however, it is best to add recipes to your menu to make up for a possible lack of food; but if time or manpower does not permit, choose recipes such as Salmon and Daikon Rolls, where it is clear that increasing amounts will not alter the delicate balance of the seasonings.

Serving appetizers at timely intervals creates an anticipation and allows you the option of serving some of the hors d'oeuvres hot from the kitchen by alternating prepared dishes (cold) with hot foods. To heat and serve saké, see Tempura Party, page 148.

The day before

1. Make Salmon and Daikon Rolls. Refrigerate, stored in an ample amount of SWEET VINEGAR.

2. Make RADISH ROSE for Chicken-stuffed Squash Balls and refrigerate, stored in sweet vinegar.

3. Cut and skewer food for Pork and Vegetable Kebabs. Refrigerate in a sealed container.

4. Prepare shrimp for Shrimp Sushi, but do not soak it. Wrap and refrigerate.

The same day

5. Begin cooking Soft Simmered Chicken Gizzards first, if using a saucepan. If using a pressure cooker, start later and time the finish accordingly, since this hors d'oeuvre requires little else after adding ingredients to pot.

6. Prepare Chicken-stuffed Squash Balls (page 44, steps 2 through 4).

7. Prepare Skewered Chicken Quenelles through step 2 (page 43).

8. Mix SAUCE for pork kebabs and lay out BREADING ingredients.

9. Retrieve shrimp for Shrimp Sushi and soak in vinegar and sugar for 10 minutes (page 47, step 1). Prepare egg and make sushi.

10. Deep-fry quenelles, kebabs (skewered the day before), and squash balls—the first two at a medium deep-frying temperature (340°F/170°C), the last at a high temperature (360°F/180°C). Bread kebabs and roll squash balls in cornstarch before deep-frying. After deep-frying, drain.

11. Skewer squash balls in tandem with radish roses; skewer quenelles together with cucumber.

To serve

12. Cut, skewer, and dab chicken gizzards with mustard.

13. Serve deep-fried appetizers hot or at room temperature.

14. Set out sauce for kebabs.

15. Remove salmon and daikon from sweet vinegar, allow to drain slightly, cut, and serve.

Yakitori Barbecue Party
Menu

• Sashimi (page 48) • Japanese-style Salad (page 100) • *Yakitori* (page 136) • Rice Balls (page 106) • "Wind in the Pines" Miso Cake (page 119)

This is an ideal menu for an outdoor barbecue party. Set up a grill and lay out platters of the tender skewered morsels on a side table. Station an assistant to grill yakitori *to order, or stand back and enjoy the fun as guests choose and cook their own kebabs.*

Party tips

The great advantage of this menu is that there is little last-minute preparation: the miso cake can be baked as early as 2 or 3 days before the event (step 1); the salad prepared the morning of the party (step 6), then refrigerated until ready to serve; the rice balls shaped and set out in a free moment (unless you specifically wish to serve them hot; step 5); and the sashimi is only a moment's work (step 7).

Fashioned into a single rose (see page 52) or even a "bouquet" of roses, garnished with leaves or green sprigs from the garden, and surrounded by plump slices of fresh fish resting invitingly on decorative beds of crisp, buoyant vegetables, tuna sashimi makes an impressive yet easy-to-make central dish for the buffet table.

Bamboo skewers are inexpensive and handy to have around. Buy twice as many as you think you will need because the actual amount of food on each skewer is less than a typical kebab, and *yakitori* is often devoured in larger quantities than expected.

Transfer your *yakitori* sauce to a nonbreakable plastic container before setting it alongside the grill. Use sauce liberally. Do not underestimate the appeal of salted *yakitori*. It is often preferred over its sweeter sauce-covered counterpart. Remember, grilled morsels should be tender, not dry.

Seven-spice mixture (*shichimi*) and *sansho* powder are worth searching for to provide variety.

The day before

1. Make miso cake. This can be done 2 or 3 days beforehand, if desired. Cover with plastic wrap and refrigerate.

2. Make YAKITORI SAUCE. Refrigerate in a sealed container. Prepare and skewer meat and vegetables. Cover with plastic wrap and refrigerate.

3. Make SESAME DRESSING for salad and refrigerate. Prepare chicken for salad.

4. Prepare GARNISHES for sashimi and refrigerate separately in airtight containers filled with fresh water.

The same day

5. Prepare plain rice and FILLINGS for rice balls. (Remember, rice must soak for at least 30 minutes before cooking and must be allowed to stand 10 to 15 minutes after it is done.) Rice balls can be eaten hot or at room temperature. To serve hot, begin preparation 1 ½ hours before serving. Otherwise, make earlier in the day, wrap in plastic or place in an airtight container, and set aside. *Do not refrigerate.*

6. Cut and arrange all salad ingredients, add dressing to custard cup, then cover and refrigerate.

7. Slice sashimi. To make sashimi rose, see page 52. For extra effect, make several roses and garnish with leaves or green sprigs from the garden. Retrieve soaking vegetables to be used as decorative beds and squeeze by hand to remove excess water. Arrange as desire. Cover with plastic wrap and refrigerate until ready to serve.

To serve

8. Set out *yakitori* alongside grill. Place sauce and salt nearby. Make guests aware of *yakitori* condiments such as seven-spice mixture or ground red pepper.

9. Bring out sashimi. Place soy sauce, *wasabi* horseradish, and a stack of small dipping dishes close at hand.

10. Serve salad. Cut cake and serve.

Intimate Sushi Party
Menu

• Shrimp and Asparagus Soup (page 38) • Green Beans with Sesame Dressing (page 98) • Thousand-layer Rolled Omelette (page 74) • Do-it-yourself Sushi (page 121) • Plum Wine Gelatin (page 117)

> *Here is a menu for an intimate sushi party that includes an appetizer (omelette), soup, salad, and Do-it-yourself Sushi—the sushi that is easiest for the host and that functions beautifully as a conversation opener, creating an immediate opportunity for guests to casually mingle as each sets out to make his or her own sushi.*

Party tips

If day-before preparations are made, then the day of the party you need only to make the sushi rice (step 7), prepare sushi ingredients (step 8), and add the finishing touches to the soup (done just before sitting down to eat; step 17).

You are ready to roll any time after the sushi rice has been tossed and cooled (step 11). This step and all the steps preceding it can be done earlier in the day. Fifteen to thirty minutes before sitting down to eat, cut and arrange omelette to be served as an hors d'oeuvre or side dish, toss salad, and set out remaining sushi ingredients (the rice will already be on the table)—small chores easily accomplished in a few minutes (steps 12 to 16). To ensure ultimate freshness, however, these last few details should be put off until the last minute or as close to the dining time as possible. Only the final preparation of the soup remains. Since the soup should be served as soon as possible after it is done and since the final two steps in the recipe take less than five minutes, time the cooking of the soup accordingly.

If desired, use sliced mushrooms or one of the other possible substitutes in place of the egg for the sushi, a practical suggestion since the rolled omelette is a close cousin anyway.

The day before

1. Make Plum Wine Gelatin. Cover with plastic wrap and refrigerate.

2. Prepare primary and secondary bonito stock. Make enough primary stock for soup and omelette, then use the same kelp and bonito flakes to make small amount of secondary stock required for salad dressing and egg for sushi.

3. Cook omelette and wrap it in a bamboo rolling mat or kitchen towel. Shape egg but do not trim or cut. Secure rolling mat or towel with rubber bands at both ends. When cool, remove mat and rubber bands and refrigerate roll.

4. Prepare egg for sushi. Cut and refrigerate.

5. Prepare shrimp for soup (page 38, steps 1 through 3), but do not boil in stock. Tightly cover with plastic wrap and refrigerate.

6. Make SESAME DRESSING for salad and cook green beans. Sprinkle green beans with *mirin* and saké. Refrigerate dressing and green beans separately.

The same day

7. Begin preparing SUSHI RICE at least 2 hours ahead of time.

8. Prepare seafood and vegetables for sushi. Finely grate ginger. Make ginger juice for soup and set aside for later use. If using powdered *wasabi*, mix paste, cover, and set aside. Attractively arrange egg for sushi (prepared the day before), seafood, vegetables, and ginger on a large serving platter, cover with plastic wrap, and refrigerate.

9. Prepare CONDIMENTS for omelette and combine daikon and cucumber. Cover and refrigerate.

10. Parboil asparagus for soup.

11. When sushi rice is done cooking, toss and cool with fan. Set it on the table in 1 or 2 serving bowls, each accompanied by enough tablespoons to allow everyone to help themselves easily. Cover with a damp cloth until ready to eat.

To serve

12. Set out soy sauce and individual dipping saucers.

13. Cut omelette, arrange pieces decoratively, garnish with sweet vinegared ginger, and set out. Set out grated daikon radish-and-cucumber mixture.

14. Mix green beans with dressing and set out.

15. Toast *nori* seaweed and cut. Place on separate plate and set on table.

16. Set out platter of sushi ingredients.

17. Finish soup. Bring bonito stock to a boil, cook shrimp, portion out all ingredients (including asparagus), and serve.

• Tuna and Cucumber with Sweet Vinegar Dressing (page 95) • Five Vegetables with Tofu Dressing (page 98) • Deep-fried Chicken Nuggets, Japanese Style (page 59) • Salmon and *Shiitake* Mushroom Sushi (page 124) • Thin Roll Sushi (page 125) • Cherry Blossom Sushi Roll (page 129) • Sushi in a Purse (page 131)

The buffet table offers few sights as mouthwatering and colorful as an abundant display of various sushis. Indulge in this extravagance for family or friends, and it will be a feast long remembered.

Party tips

Sushis can be made a half day ahead of time, covered with plastic wrap, and set aside, unrefrigerated. However, sashimi-filled or -topped sushis should not be made any earlier than an hour before you are ready to serve, though sashimi may be trimmed and cut (then returned to the refrigerator) for quick rolling or shaping later on. Similarly, be cautious with other seafood if the weather is particularly sultry.

If your guest list begins growing at the last minute or you have suspicions that guests will be unusually ravenous, add Do-it-yourself Sushi (page 121), setting out as much filling as you deem necessary.

The two dressed foods ("salads") suggested here are useful to stimulate appetites. Serve already portioned in individual bowls or on dessert plates (or serve each salad in a serving bowl with small spoons to suggest petit portions). Set out an ample amount of sweet vinegared ginger (see page 27), which refreshes the palate between mouthfuls of sushi.

The day before

1. Prepare mushrooms and gourd ribbons for four sushi recipes and mushrooms for Five Vegetables with Tofu Dressing. To save time, cook together, adjusting seasoning to taste. (Do not forget gourd ribbon "purse strings" for Sushi in a Purse, if not using spinach.)

2. Prepare secondary bonito stock for vegetables to be used in salad (or use water and skip this step).

3. Cut chicken and combine with MARINADE. Cover and refrigerate overnight. Decrease amount of soy sauce slightly.

4. Prepare carrot, cucumber, thin deep-fried tofu (*aburage*) and green beans for Five Vegetables with Tofu Dressing (page 99, steps 2 through 5). If using apple, do not add until later (see step 22). Mix vegetables (including mushrooms) and deep-fried tofu. Cover and refrigerate.

5. Make SWEET VINEGAR DRESSING for tuna and cucumber salad.

6. Parboil spinach for Cherry Blossom Sushi Roll and Sushi in a Purse (if not using gourd ribbons as purse strings).

7. Prepare turnips for salmon and mushroom sushi.

8. Prepare shrimp, snow peas, and carrot for Sushi in a Purse. Wrap and refrigerate both shrimp and snow peas separately. Chop mushrooms and gourd ribbons and mix with carrots slivers. Cover and refrigerate.

The same day

9. Prepare SUSHI RICE. You may want to make it in two batches, cooking the second batch while you are making sushi with the first batch. If so, begin cooking first batch at least 4 to 5 hours ahead of time to allow yourself plenty of leeway.

10. Make TOFU DRESSING for salad and refrigerate.

11. Cook egg sheets for Sushi in a Purse.

12. Prepare egg and lettuce for Salmon and *Shiitake* Mushroom Sushi.

13. Prepare tuna and cucumber for Thin Roll Sushi and refrigerate.

14. Prepare *wasabi* horseradish for salmon sushi and Thin Roll Sushi. Make 1 cup dilute vinegar to moisten hands by mixing ½ cup water with ½ cup rice vinegar.

15. When sushi rice is done, begin assembling sushi. Make Sushi in a Purse first. Trim egg sheets, toast sesame seeds, and retrieve vegetables (mushrooms, gourd ribbons, carrots, snow peas, and spinach or gourd ribbons for purse strings) prepared the day before. Toss with correct amount of sushi rice and then assemble sushi. As a guide, remember that 1 cup uncooked rice makes approximately 2 cups cooked rice.

16. Assemble Salmon and Mushroom Sushi next. Cut mushroom caps diagonally into 3 pieces, cut salmon, and assemble. Remember, only salmon takes *wasabi* horseradish.

17. Make small pink sushi roll "blossoms" and then assemble Cherry Blossom Sushi.

18. With remaining sushi rice, make Thin Roll Sushi. Remember, gourd ribbons do not take *wasabi* horseradish.

19. Heat oil, add egg white and cornstarch to chicken, and deep-fry. Cut and deep-fry bell peppers. Arrange and set out.

To serve

20. Set out soy sauce and individual dipping saucers.

21. Combine canned tuna, cucumber, oil from tuna, and sweet vinegar dressing, following recipe steps 3 through 5.

22. Prepare apple for Five Vegetables with Tofu Dressing (if not using *aburage*). Combine all ingredients with dressing and serve.

Tempura Party
Menu

• Clear Soup with Chicken and Okra (page 37) • Crab and Cucumber with Golden Dressing (page 96) • Tempura (page 138) • Plain Rice (page 101) • Lemony Pickled Turnips (page 115) • Strawberries in Bubbles of Snow (page 118)

Tempura—with its delicate, lacy coating—adds a special elegance to any meal or party, and the dainty Strawberries in Bubbles of Snow gracefully concludes this repast.

Party tips

Two of the six dishes (the pickles and the dessert) can be completed the day before the party, and a third (rice) requires only cooking—no adornment or further preparation. The salad dressing and the chicken for the soup are also prepared the previous day.

The day of the party, small chores will take up only a small portion of your time. Once these are accomplished, cooking the tempura and serving the food are all that remain.

The nature of tempura does not allow for cooking ahead of time. In fact, it should not be cooked until guests are settled in and ready to eat, and then it should be served immediately. Start the meal off with soup, salad, pickles, and drink. This will keep the guests occupied while the tempura is cooking. The soup can also be served afterward.

An assistant will speed things up, and an extra skillet for deep-frying the tempura is also a good idea. If you choose, display the fresh ingredients and let each guest put in his or her own order after surveying the fresh foods.

Saké is an excellent accompaniment. Keep a pot of boiling water ready, fill small saké carafes with saké, and heat in boiling water. Saké carafes will not be damaged in the process; they are designed with this purpose in mind. Saké can also be heated in a microwave oven, which heats saké in 1 to 2 minutes.

The day before

1. Pickle turnips the day before the party or as early as 3 days before. Refrigerate, uncut, in an airtight container.

2. Make dessert. Refrigerate uncut.

3. Prepare primary bonito stock for soup and secondary bonito stock for tempura and salad. Refrigerate.

4. Boil DIPPING SAUCE for tempura. Refrigerate, stored in sealed bottle.

5. Combine ingredients for GOLDEN DRESSING. Cover and refrigerate.

6. Prepare chicken for soup (page 38, step 1).

The same day

7. Prepare seafood for deep-frying. Refrigerate.

8. Begin preparing rice at least an hour in advance.

9. Make crab and cucumber for salad. Refrigerate undressed.

10. Remove chicken and tempura dipping sauce from refrigerator. Let them warm to room temperature. Just before serving tempura, heat dipping sauce until luke warm, if desired.

11. Cut vegetables and grate CONDIMENTS for tempura. Cut okra for soup.

To serve

12. Heat oil for tempura. While oil is heating, do steps 13 through 16.

13. Finish soup by bringing bonito stock to a boil and adding ingredients as directed (page 38, step 3). Serve.

14. Cut dessert.

15. Set out rice, salad (with dressing), and pickles.

16. Make tempura BATTER.

17. Fry tempura, serving it immediately.

Mixed Grill Party

Menu

- Miso Soup with Tofu and *Wakame* Seaweed (page 39) • Fresh Tuna and Green Onion with Miso and Vinegar Dressing (page 96) • Mixed Grill (page 66) • Green Pea Rice (page 104) • Cucumber Pickles (page 115) • Twice-cooked Egg Cake (page 120)

> *The keynote here is ease for the host. Since the preparation of ingredients to be grilled is a small matter and since the soup and "salad" are quickly accomplished, this menu is ideal when, on short notice, one suddenly finds oneself called upon to fill in as host.*

Party tips

Since guests choose and grill their own foods, the burden that traditionally falls to the host is lightened, his or her most important task then being to select appropriate ingredients to be grilled.

When gathering ingredients for Mixed Grill, include some known favorites of your prospective guests. Select fresh seasonal vegetables and seafood and add any seasonal delicacy, if desired. Cut and arrange them artfully with ingredients almost spilling over the edge of the serving platter to suggest plenitude and sumptuousness, and guests cannot help but be impressed.

Plan on one electric griddle (or skillet on a tabletop unit) for every four diners. With this type of meal, oil may splatter, so provide bibs (as is often done in restaurants that serve spare ribs and other finger food), or large paper or cloth napkins. Make sure you have an ample supply of both dipping sauces on hand.

The pickle side dish, the cake, the salad dressing, and the two sauces for Mixed Grill are prepared the day before the event (steps 1 through 5). Same-day preparations are few and simple: cook Green Pea Rice, cut ingredients for Mixed Grill, prepare main ingredients for soup and salad, and toast and grind sesame seeds (steps 6 through 9). When you are ready to serve, heat electric griddle, set out dipping sauces and platters of fresh ingredients for grilling, and let guests begin. While diners are grilling the foods of their choice, add the finishing touches to the soup and salad (steps 12 and 13) and serve.

The day before

1. Make Cucumber Pickles. Cover and refrigerate.

2. Make Twice-cooked Egg Cake. Cover and refrigerate, uncut.

3. Make secondary bonito stock for miso soup, Mixed Grill (used in SESAME SAUCE), and tuna salad (used in dressing).

4. Make MISO AND VINEGAR DRESSING for salad.

5. Make LEMON-SOY DIP and SESAME SAUCE for Mixed Grill, but do not toast sesame seeds until step 9. Refrigerate in sealed containers.

The same day

6. Begin Green Pea Rice 1½ to 2 hours before sitting down to eat.

7. Prepare meat, seafood, and vegetables for grilling (page 67, step 1). Arrange on several serving platters, cover with plastic wrap, and refrigerate.

8. Prepare green onion and tuna for salad (page 97, steps 1 and 2), but do not combine. Prepare *wakame* seaweed and tofu for soup.

9. Toast and grind sesame seed for Mixed Grill's sesame sauce. Combine with sauce prepared the day before.

To serve

10. Set out Cucumber Pickles.

11. Set out platters of Mixed Grill ingredients. Heat electric griddle and begin grilling. Provide lemon-soy dip and sesame sauce for each diner.

12. Finish soup (page 39, steps 2 through 4). Serve.

13. Combine tuna, green onion, and dressing. Serve.

14. Cut cake and serve.

Oriental Food Shops in the United States

ALABAMA

Chai's Oriental Foods
2133 7th Avenue South
Birmingham 35216

Ebino's Oriental Foods
323 Airbase Blvd
Montgomery 36108

Oriental Market
5 Point Sak Hwy 431 N
Anniston 36201

Oriental Supermarket
2751 Pleasant Vy Rd
Mobile 36606

Su-Ki Oriental Grocery
2701-C Patton Rd
Huntsville 35805

CALIFORNIA *

Asahi Company
660 Oxnard Blvd
Oxnard 93030

Asian Foods
4555 N Pershing #14
Stockton 95207

Berkeley Bowl
2777 Shattuck Ave
Berkeley 94705

Dobashi Market
240 Jackson St
San Jose 95112

Ebisu Market
18940 Brookhurst St
Fountain Valley 92708

Eiko Shoten
6082 University Ave
San Diego 90502

Enbun Co
248 E 1st St
Los Angeles 90012

Fuji Store
353 E Washington St
Petaluma 94952

Fujiya Market
601 N Virgil Ave
Los Angeles 90004

Fukuda's
2412 S Escondido Blvd
Escondido 92025

Futaba Food Center
1507 Lincoln Ave
Pasadena 91103

Hong's Market
300 Carmel Ave
Marina 93933

Maruwa Foods Co, Inc
1737 Post Street
San Francisco 94115

Mihama Fish Market
2601 Pacific Coast Hwy
Torrance 90505

Miyako Oriental Fd Inc
404 Towne Ave
Los Angeles 90013

Modern Food Market
601 West Anaheim St
Wilmington 90744

Motoyama Market
16135 S Western Ave
Gardena 90247

Newark Market
36601 Newark Blvd
Newark 94560

Nippon Food Market
2935 Ball Rd
Anaheim 92804

Omori's
2700 N Santa Fe
Vista 92083

Parlier Fish Market
PO Box 189
Parlier 93648

Sakae Oriental Grocery
4227 Convoy St
San Diego 92111

Senri Fish Market
111 N Lincoln Ave
Monterey Park 91754

Suruki Oriental Food
1360 Broadway
Burlingame 94010

Takahashi Co
221 S Claremont
San Mateo 94401

Tokyo Oriental Fd Mkt
San Miguel Ave
Salinas 93901

Uoki
1656 Post St
San Francisco 94115

Williams Bros #15
1650 Grand Ave
Arroyo Grande 93420

Willow Mini Mart
3185 Willow Avenue
Clovis 93612

Yamasaki Grocery
1566 Santa Fe Ave
Long Beach 90813

COLORADO

Ann's Oriental Grocery
315 Arvada Street
Colorado Springs 80906

Granada Fish Market
1275 19th Street
Denver 80202

Kim Young Oriental
1444 Chester St
Aurora 80010

Pacific Mercantile
1925 Lawrence St
Denver 80202

Park's Oriental Market
229 N Academy Blvd
Colorado Springs 80909

CONNECTICUT

China Trading Co
271 Crown St
New Haven 06510

East/West Trading Co
68 Howe Street
New Haven 06511

Kim's Oriental Fd
202 Park Road
W Hartford 06119

Young's Oriental Groc
243 Farmington Ave
Hartford 06105

DELAWARE

Newark Oriental
174 Elkton Rd
Newark 19711

Oriental Grocery
1705 Concord Pike
Wilmington 19803

Young's Oriental
2011 Kirkwood Hwy
Wilmington 19805

FLORIDA

Aberdeen Foods
631 S Dixie Hwy East
Pompano Beach 33060

Aloha Foods & Gift
3284 N State Rd 7
Lauderdale Lake 33309

Fujiya Japanese Market
12777 79th SW 280th St
Homestead 33030

Japanese Market
1412 NE 79th St Cswy
North Bay Village

Misako's Oriental Fd
129 New Warrington Rd
North Pensacola 32406

Nobuko's Far Est Bazaar
73 Sailfish Dr
Atlantic Beach 32233

Oriental Food Store
4559 Shirley Ave
Jacksonville 32210

Oriental Import
1118 South Orange Ave
Orlando

Oriental Market
1202 S Dale Mabry Hwy
Tampa 33609

Tomiko's Japnse Fd
441 Bryn Athyn
Mary Esther 32569

Yates Brothers Inc
4601 Hines Rd
St Petersburg 33714

GEORGIA

Asian Supermarket
2581 Piedmont Rd
Atlanta 30324

Kimlon Oriental Foods
341 North Cobb Hwy
Marietta 30062

Makoto's Japanese Fd
1067 Oaktree Rd
Decatur 30033

Nippon-Daido Co
2390 Carroll Ave
Chamblee 30341

Oakland Park Ort'l Fd
2031 South Lumpkin Rd
Columbus 31903

Oriental Food Store
3082 Deansbridge Rd
Augusta 30906

Satsuma-ya
5271-B Buford Hwy
Doraville 30340

---

*Japanese foods are also available at selected locations of many
supermarket chains, including Albertson's, Alpha Beta, Foods Co,
Hughes Markets, Lucky Stores, Pioneer Foods, Ralph's, and Von's.

151

IDAHO

Yuko's Gift
688 N Holmes Ave
Idaho Falls 83401

ILLINOIS

Berry's Store
1702 Harrison
Quincy 62301

Chang's Ort'l Fd
5214–16 N Lincoln Ave
Chicago 60625

Clark Market
570 E Algonquin Road
Des Plaines 60016

Co-op Supermarket
1526 East 55th Street
Chicago 60615

Dempster Plaza Ort'l
8828 West Dempster St
Niles 60648

Far East Ort'l Food
1524 Grand Ave
Waukegan 60085

Furuya & Company
5358 N Clark St
Chicago 60640

Golden Country Store
2422 Wentworth Ave
Chicago 60616

Hisaye's Oriental Food
112 Homestead
O'Fallon 62269

House of Orient
434 S Washington St
Naperville 60540

J Toguri Mercantile
851 W Belmont Ave
Chicago 60657

Kyotoya Corp Fd & Crft
1182 S Elmhurst
Mt Prospect 60056

Lin's International
1537 S State St
Chicago 60605

M & S Oriental Fd Mart
2208 Bloomingdale Rd
Glendale Heights 60137

Mayjean Co
1806 Irving Park Road
Hanover Park 60103

Medical Center Fd Mart
1926 W Harrison Ave
Chicago 60612

Mieko Rickman Ginza
315 E University
Champaign 61820

Ort'l Store of Chicago
1804 W Irving Park Rd
Chicago 60613

Oriental Treasure Ctr
675 N Cass Ave
Westmont 60559

Ramel's Food Store
932 Madison St
Oak Park 60302

Schaumburg Oriental
710 East Higgins Road
Schaumburg 60195

Shinanoya Market
940 W Algonquin Road
Arlington Hts 60005

Silahis Oriental
648 Meacham Rd
Elk Grove Vil 60007

Skokie Oriental
3922 Dempster
Skokie 60076

Waukegan Ort'l Store
2859 Washington St
Waukegan 60085

Westchester Ort'l Fd
10024 Roosevelt Rd
Westchester 60153

INDIANA

Asia Oriental Market
2400 Yeager Rd
W Lafayette 47906

Indy Ort'l Grocery
6430 E Washington St
Indianapolis 46224

Orient Food Mart
4677 W 30th St
Indianapolis 46224

IOWA

Jung's Oriental Fd
913 E University Ave
Des Moines 50316

KANSAS

Oriental Import
310 Grant Ave
Junction City 66441

KENTUCKY

Oriental Foods & Gift
357 South Land Drive
Lexington 40503

Reiko Ort'l Fd & Gft
2613 Frederica St
Ownesboro 42301

LOUISIANA

Korea House
Rt 5 Box 268
Leesville 71446

MARYLAND

Asia House
1576 Annapolis Rd
Odenton 21113

Far East Import
1902 Pulaski Hwy
Edgewood 21040

Fumi Oriental Mart
2102 Viers Mill Rd
Rockville 20852

Jade Tree
350 Fortune Terrace
Potomac 20854

K Oriental
7151 Security Blvd
Baltimore 21207

Maxim Market
646 University Blvd
Silver Spring 20903

MASSACHUSETTS

House of Kim
852 Massachusetts Ave
Lexington 02173

Joyce Chen Unlimited
172 Massachusetts Ave
Arlington 02174

Mirim Trading Co Inc
152 Harvard Ave
Allston 02134

See Sun Co
36 Harrison St
Boston 02111

Yoshinoya
36 Prospect Street
Cambridge 02139

MICHIGAN

Chun's Store
112 Quincy
Hancock 49930

Sing Tong Int'l Food
1510 North Maple
Ann Arbor 48103

Tropical Food Mart
4638 Woodward Ave
Detroit 48201

MINNESOTA

Grocers' Supply Inc
860 Vandalia
St Paul 55114

Kim's Ort'l Grocery
689 N Snelling Ave
St Paul 55104

Oriental Plaza
607 Cedar Ave
Minneapolis 55454

Phil Ort'l Imports
476 N Lexington Pkwy
St Paul 55104

MISSISSIPPI

Oriental Mart
102 Wilmington St
Jackson 39204

MISSOURI

Fuji Snack Bar
Rt 6 Box 100
Waynesville

Kim's Mart
6692 Enright
St Louis 63130

NEW JERSEY

Aki Oriental Food Co
1635 Lemoine Ave
Fort Lee 07024

Asian Food Market
217 Summit Ave
Jersey City 07306

Chiari Store
Hwy #77 Road
Brigeton 08302

Miyako Oriental Foods
490 Main St
Ft Lee 07024

Rice Bowl
1636-3 North King Hwy
Cherry Hill 08034

NEW MEXICO

Fremont Fine Foods
556 Coronado Cn NE
Albuquerque 87110

Yonemoto Bros
8725 Fourth Street NW
Albuquerque 87114

NEW YORK

Ajiya Mart Inc
41–75 Bowne St
Flushing 11354

Daido
41-54 Main St
Flushing 11355

Five Continental Foods
80–19 Broadway El
Elmhurst 11373

Global Food
80–06 Roosevelt Ave
Jackson Heights 11372

Harumi
318–320 W 231 St
Bronx 10463

Jack Yuen Trading Co
56 E Broadway
New York 10002

Katagiri Company
224 East 59th St
New York 10022

Kim's Oriental Groc
4311 E Genesee St
Dewitt 13214

Kim's Oriental Shoppe
1649 Central Ave
Albany 12205

Koramerica Co Inc
127 West 43rd St
New York 10036

Lee's Oriental Foods
11 Pullman Ave
Rochester 14615

Meidiya
18 N Central Park Ave
Hartsdale 10530

New World Corporation
103-37 Queens Blvd
Forest Hill 11375

Nippon Do
82-69 Parsons Blvd
Jamaica 11432

Oh Bok Oriental Mart
1772 Forest Ave
Staten Island 10302

Oriental Groc & Prd
2460 Nesconset Hwy
Stonybrook 11790

Queens Ort'l Fd & Gft
81-02 Broadway
Elmhurst 11373

Shin Shin Market
142-01 38th Ave
Flushing 11355

Sunnyside Oriental Fd
47-01 Queens Blvd
Sunnyside 11104

Tanaka & Company
326 Amsterdam Ave
New York 10023

Tokyo Sales Corp
142 W 57th St
New York 10019

Tomon
5678 Mosholu Ave
Bronx 10471

Tsujimoto Oriental
Art Gifts & Food Inc
6530 Seneca, Elma

NORTH CAROLINA

Chang's Oriental Fd
7430 North Tryon St
Charlotte 28036

Kim's Oriental Foods
19 Haywood St
Ashville 28801

Oriental Food Mart
803 N Main St
Spring Lake 28390

Ort'l Store of Raleigh
3121 North Blvd
Raleigh 27604

Riddle Oriental
4405 Wrightsville Ave
Wilmington 28403

Silver Wok
200 North Greensboro
Carboro 27510

OHIO

Firelands Cntry Str
RT 113
Amherst 44001

Omura Japnse Fd & Gft
3811 Payne Ave
Cleveland 44114

Oriental Food & Gifts
500 W Main St
Fairborn 45324

Overbey's Emporium
6072 Busch Blvd
Columbus 43229

Soya Food Products
2356 Wyoming Ave
Cincinnati 45214

OREGON

Anzen Imports
736 NE Union Ave
Portland 97232

PENNSYLVANIA

Asian Grocery
6458 Market St
Upper Darby 19082

Choice Super Mkt
4357 New Fall Rd
Levittown 19056

Internat'l Super Mkt
117 North 10th St
Philadelphia 19107

Moo Koong Wha
30 North York Rd
Willow Grove 19090

Sambok Market
1737 Penn Ave
Pittsburgh 15222

Zi-on
17 West 2nd Street
Lansdale 19446

RHODE ISLAND

East Sea Oriental Mkt
90-92 Warren Ave
E Providence 02914

Persimmon Oriental Mkt
University Hts Shop Cn
Providence 02906

SOUTH CAROLINA

Chieko Hardy Japns Fd
226 Jamaica St
Columbia 29206

Oriental Food & Gift
4252 Rivers Ave
North Charleston 29405

Sachi's Oriental Groc
54 Brabham Dr
Dalzell 29040

SOUTH DAKOTA

Kitty's Oriental Food
PO Box 347
Box Elder 57719

TENNESSEE

Asia House Oriental Fd
4501 Kingston Pike SW
Knoxville 37917

Cherry Blossom Shop
1823 Memorial NS PL
Murefreesboro 37130

Import Shop
1775 Fort Henry Dr
Kingsport 37664

Kay's Oriental Food
1509 Ft Campbell Blvd
Clarksville 37040

Orient Foods
1513 Church St
Nashville 37203

Pan East Mercantile
110 Randolph Grove Cn
Oak Ridge 37830

Sun Oriental Food
4446 Summer Avenue
Memphis 38122

TEXAS

Airport Fina Co
502 Pampa Dr
Austin 78752

Edoya Oriental
232 Farmers Branch
Dallas 75234

Equelet Grocery
3623 Red Bluff
Pasadena 77503

New Orient Rest & Sply
108 Ave D West
Killeen 76541

Nippon Daido Int'l
11138 Westheimer
Houston 77042

Northside Oriental Mkt
2024 Bandera Rd
San Antonio 78228

Numis Ports Oriental
PO Drawer A
Alvin 77511

The Oriental
809 University Ave
Lubbock 79401

Sahadi Imported Foods
713 N 10th St
McAllen 78501

Yamamoto Grocery
3103 Fondren Rd
Houston 77063

VIRGINIA

China Grocery Inc
3509 S Jefferson St
Baileys Crossroad

Han Yang Oriental
4251 Annandale Cn Dr
Annandale 22003

Oriental House
7816 Richmond Hwy
Alexandria 22306

Sam-mi
6674 Arlington Blvd
Falls Church 22042

Super Asian Market
2719 Wilson Blvd
Arlington 22201

Tokyo Market
7528 Granby St
Norfolk 23505

Toyo Market
5312 Virginia Boh Blvd
Virginia Beach 23462

WASHINGTON

Uwajimaya, Inc
6th St & S King St
Seattle 98104

WASHINGTON, D.C.

Da Hua Foods Inc
6171 I Street NW
20001

Hiroshima
7838 Eastern Ave
20012

Mikado
4709 Wisconsin Ave
NW 20016

Wang's Co
800 7th St NW
20001

WISCONSIN

Oriental Shop
1029 South Park St
Madison 53715

Peace Oriental Foods
4250 W Fond Du Lac
Ave Milwaukee 53216

Index

定価2,900円
in Japan